ANNA RITCHIE

CW01646114

SCOTLAND BC

AN INTRODUCTION TO THE PREHISTORIC HOUSES, TOMBS, CEREMONIAL MONUMENTS AND FORTIFICATIONS IN THE CARE OF THE SCOTTISH MINISTERS

I do love these ancient ruins:
We never tread upon them, but we set
Our foot upon some reverend history . . .

John Webster, *The Duchess of Malfi* (c 1614)

HISTORIC SCOTLAND

Contents

Note: Those monuments in state care mentioned in the book are shown in **bold** type. Reference to any other site does not imply public access.

Edited by Christopher Tabraham
Principal photography by David Henrie
Historic Scotland Photographic Unit

First Published by HMSO 1988
This edition published by Historic Scotland 1999

ISBN 1 900168 79 0

Front Cover

"*Druidical Temple at Tormore, Isle of Arran*" by William Andrews Nesfield, reproduced by courtesy of the Victoria and Albert Museum.

Nesfield exhibited this water colour at the Society of Painters in Water-Colours in 1828. The standing stones depicted are from the Machrie Moor group whose accurate location is adjacent to the Moor, on Tormore Moss.

Back Cover

A ceremonial stone macehead on a modern wooden haft (c 2500 BC).

Inside Front Cover

Dun Carloway, Lewis

The people of Carloway have lived in the comforting shadow of their broch for 2000 years — it was used as a refuge even in medieval times. It is magnificently sited, its walls flowing into the rocky outcrop on which it stands so that it is difficult to see where nature ends and artifice begins.

Opposite

Balnuaran of Clava, Inverness

Sheltered by trees, the megalithic cemetery at **Clava** is a still and powerful place, retaining immense dignity after some 4000 years.

Uncovering prehistory: excavations underway at **Knap of Howar.**

Prehistoric architecture has been particularly vulnerable to stone-robbing: the great **Grey Cairn of Camster** in Caithness has a humped profile partly as a result of having been used as a quarry for stones to build field-walls or the sheep-fold in the foreground.

Time is relative: this neolithic carved stone ball was treasured as a curiosity some 3000 years later by someone living in the Dark Age fort of **Dunadd,** near Lochgilphead in Argyll, just as we collect and treasure the artefacts of Dark Age times.

EIGHT hundred years separate us from Bjorn, who carved his name in runes on one of the great standing stones of the **Ring of Brodgar** in Orkney. Four thousand years separated Bjorn from the people who laboured to quarry the stones and set them up. The circle that they created was to dominate their landscape as later it dominated Bjorn's and as it still does today, and in that sense the stones become a link between some 170 generations. Yet the role that the stones played has changed, from being the focus of ceremony for their original builders to being an object of wonder in the modern world — Bjorn added a Christian cross beneath his name, perhaps in an effort to curb the pagan splendour of the place.

This combination of being a direct link with the remote past and of playing a changing role in the landscape is a vital aspect of the wide range of prehistoric monuments in the care of the Secretary of State for Scotland. In some cases excavation during the last century has revealed a monument worthy of preservation, but most of the antiquities in this book have been a permanent and visible component of the landscape, even if their date and meaning have been little understood until recent times. Some have been used as convenient sources of building stone (brochs in particular have suffered this way), while others have increased in size as stones cleared from the arable fields around them have been dumped on top. Their impact upon the community can often be appreciated through placenames and folklore: **Ness of Burgi** in Shetland has been known as 'promontory of the fort' at least since the Viking Age (Old Norse *ness*, promontory, and *borg*, fort), and the **Dwarfie Stane** on Hoy in Orkney found its way as an elven residence both into local folklore and into national literature in Sir Walter Scott's novel *The Pirate*.

The range of monuments in state care includes most major classes of archaeological structures, some donated by landowners and others purchased. The importance of protecting a sample of the Scottish heritage has been recognised in this way since the first monument, the **White Caterthun** fort in Angus, was taken into guardianship in 1884. Excavation has been used as a means of discovering the date and purpose of a structure, as well as tidying it up for display, but total excavation is a destructive process and a choice often has to be made between excavation and preservation.

Humans have been a modifying factor in the Scottish environment for at least 9000 years, but they left few traces for the first 3000 years. The camp-sites of people whose livelihoods depended upon fishing, hunting, and collecting wild plants, berries and nuts rarely leave more than the debris of hearths and stone-working. It was only after the introduction of a more settled, farming life-style around 4000 BC that people began to build permanent houses and burial-places, thereby making a lasting mark on the landscape. The extent to which these survive above ground depends primarily upon the materials used to build them: wood rots away, leaving only the holes dug to hold the upright timbers, whereas a stone wall, left alone, can survive indefinitely. Excavation at Balbridie, beside the River Dee in Aberdeenshire, uncovered the post-holes of what must have been a magnificent wooden house, fully 24.5 m long and 13 m wide, in which people were living around 3600 BC. This date, like others used in this book, is based upon scientific analysis of charcoal or bone found during excavation: by measuring the radioactive carbon surviving in the sample, it is possible to estimate how long ago the tree or animal was living. These radiocarbon years can then be converted to calendar years.

The Old Red Sandstone bedrock of Orkney splits easily along its bedding planes to produce rectangular slabs ideal for building: thick slabs for walls, thin slabs for partitions and roofing.

Nothing of the Balbridie house could be seen at ground level because its timbers had rotted away, and there must have been many other such wooden houses built throughout prehistoric times in the forests of north-east Scotland. Elsewhere, lack of good timber made stone the natural choice for building — in some cases, especially in Orkney, the high quality and easy availability of the local stone may even have made it the preferred choice — and many stone buildings survive above ground level from 5000 or more years ago. The best-preserved houses of this early period, at **Knap of Howar** and **Skara Brae** in Orkney, were protected over the centuries by a blanket of sand, but even without such protection stone walls can survive as low banks outlining the original house.

Outside Orkney it was not always possible to achieve such excellence in drystone masonry, simply because of the variable quality of local stone. In Shetland, for example, well-bedded sandstone was available at **Jarlshof**, whereas further north at **Stanydale** and on Whalsay the

Along the fertile western shore of Rousay, the chambered tombs are spaced out as if their neolithic owners had shared out the land in the same parcels as those of more recent farms. There are four tombs in state care along this stretch: **Midhowe, Yarso, Blackhammer** and **Taversoe Tuick,** and several others not so well preserved.

use of rounded boulders brought problems of stability. The answer lay in very thick walls with huge stones at their base, creating a truly megalithic architecture. The collapsed remains of such walls can be misleading: one of the neolithic houses at Pettigarth's Field on Whalsay was known locally as the 'Standing Stones of Yoxie' because of the huge boulders protruding from its walls. A similar effect led to the identification of a house at **Steinacleit** on Lewis as a chambered tomb.

Permanent buildings and a settled farming economy characterise the period from 3800 BC; known to archaeologists as the neolithic period, the next 1000 years and more have left us houses and field-walls, tombs, stone-carvings, ceremonial circles of earth and stone, and a wide range of equipment from pottery to bone and stone tools. What survives is of course only a partial record and much is missing. Many items must have been made of organic materials that rot away, unless exceptional soil conditions preserve them: wooden bowls and platters, harpoons and ploughs, leather bags, shoes and clothes, baskets woven from heather twigs. These we can assume from common sense and necessity. We can deduce that clothes were made from animal skins rather than textiles because no spinning or weaving equipment has been found from this period and the primitive sheep bore hair rather than proper wool suitable for yarn.

What of the wider issues of social life? Interpreting these carries the danger of applying modern values and experience to remote societies, but nevertheless a justifiable outline can be seen. A sense of community emerges from what we know of neolithic people : basic ideas of how the dead should be buried and how their tombs should be built were shared over wide areas of Britain, as were fashions in pottery, and tombs were communal, used for successive burials over hundreds of years, rather than individual, once only, graves. Contact between communities can be seen in the long-distance exchange networks demonstrated by the distribution of stone axes, products from axe factories in the English Lake District and County Antrim in Northern Ireland being found, for instance, on Scottish sites.

The building of even the smallest family tomb or farmhouse needed organisation, and, by the time that massive public monuments such as stone circles were being undertaken in the 3rd millennium BC, this organisation must have taken the form of a stratified tribal society, in which there was a strong sense of group identity. The introduction of metal working from about 2000 BC marks the beginning not only of a new technology, allowing more sophisticated jewellery, tools, and weapons made of bronze, but also of the dominance of the individual in society. Communal burial was replaced by individual burial, and, instead of communal offerings to the dead, each burial was furnished with its own, personal gravegoods. Such burials record the status of powerful individuals in society, people such as chieftains, priests, and bronzesmiths.

An important factor lies behind these social developments: climate. The introduction of farming took place under the best possible conditions for Scotland, during a period when the climate was relatively warm and dry compared to earlier and later times. Throughout the neolithic period, the range of temperatures was similar to that of today and the average temperature was slightly higher. It was warm enough to grow wheat as well as barley in the Northern Isles, and sea temperatures were warm enough to encourage fish such as red sea bream and corkwing wrasse to inhabit northern seas that they shun today. The picture is not entirely rosy, because wind speeds seem to have increased around 3000 BC, leading eventually to the formation of sand-dunes in northern Scotland, but nevertheless the overall climate encouraged mixed farming and the development of a stable life-style. Successful farming meant sufficient food to store and the release of labour for ambitious communal building projects, as well as the development of a stratified society within which such projects could be organised.

In contrast to the plantations of sitka spruce that make up many of today's new forests, the natural forests of 5000 years ago were pinewoods or a fine mixture of oak, willow, alder and birch that provided the raw materials for many needs, from logboats hewn from great oak trunks to drains lined with birch bark. Thus axe and adze were essential tools for tree felling and the treatment of timber, whether made of stone as in neolithic times or of bronze as in the 2nd millennium BC.

The beginning of the 2nd millennium, around 2000 BC, brought major changes, at least in the archaeological record: individual burials replaced communal tombs; cremation became as acceptable a rite as inhumation; a new pottery fashion, the beaker, appeared; and, above all, metallurgy in the form of copper, bronze, and gold working was introduced. But the old was not entirely forsaken by the new. The potency of the long-established sacred landscapes remained

This graceful type of pottery vessel is known as a beaker and is often beautifully decorated.

Cup-and-ring marks carved on a bare rock-face at **Ballygowan**, Argyll.

powerful: the **Ring of Brodgar** in Orkney became a focus for burial mounds of the 2nd millennium and the **Kilmartin** valley in Argyll continued to attract important burials and alignments of standing stones, as well as stimulating such extraordinary displays of rock-art as that at **Ballygowan**.

Both the beaker style of pottery and the art of metalworking were entirely new ideas that originated in continental Europe. It is still a matter of discussion amongst archaeologists as to whether these new ideas were carried across the North Sea by immigrant settlers or whether they spread by trade or exchange between communities; although full-scale invasion is certainly unlikely, it seems probable that some new people, especially craftsmen, were involved. By comparing the shape and decorative styles of beakers in Britain and Europe, it is possible to pinpoint the Lower Rhine basin as one of the areas from which beakers were introduced into Scotland.

Traces of settlements at this period are more elusive in the archaeological record than funerary monuments, and the 2nd millennium BC might appear to have been dominated by death if it were not for the abundant products of the bronzesmith. Future excavations are likely to alter this one-sided picture, because surface fieldwork in upland areas such as Perthshire has identified hut-circles and field-systems that could well prove to be of this period.

Towards the end of the 2nd millennium BC, the climate throughout Britain began to worsen, becoming colder and wetter and encouraging the growth of peat. This meant that cultivation was more difficult, with crops more likely to fail, and that less arable land was available — together with changing social factors, the result was a distinct pressure on communities to protect their livelihood and themselves from others who may have been on the brink of starvation. The archaeological record betrays a society depending increasingly on weapons and turning to defensive measures to protect its homes. In Scotland the building of hillforts was underway in the 7th century BC and even small farms were enclosed by stout timber stockades, although unenclosed settlements were also used at this period.

By the middle of the 1st millennium, the use of iron for hardier tools and weapons was taking over from bronze, though the latter remained in use, particularly for jewellery. The role of the blacksmith was to become very important in Celtic society. To what extent Celtic immigrants were involved in these developments is a matter for conjecture: timber-lacing, a method of reinforcing the walls and ramparts of forts, was certainly first developed in north-west Europe among the Celts, as was iron-working, but innovations can be spread by only a few people and need not imply any mass movement of population. Language is a surer indicator of change in the make-up of a population, and there is certainly linguistic evidence of a Celtic-speaking population in Scotland long before the Romans arrived in the 1st century AD. Until recently, it was assumed that the Celtic language was introduced by Celtic immigrants from the 7th century BC onwards, but Professor Colin Renfrew has argued persuasively that the spread of Indo-European languages, of which Celtic was one, could have occurred alongside the spread of farming several millennia earlier. For Scotland, this would have taken place from about 4000 BC. If Renfrew is right, there is no need to invoke more than a minor influx of Celts to account for the introduction of timber-laced forts in the 7th century BC — warlords, perhaps, seeking new lands.

Timber-laced forts can be dated by radiocarbon analysis of their wooden beams, but it is otherwise very difficult to date fortifications built of stone or earth and rubble, as finds tend to be scarce even on excavated sites. Surface fieldwork and aerial survey can suggest relative sequences on sites with a long structural history, such as **Edin's Hall** in Berwickshire.

Few Scottish hillforts are as large as many of their English counterparts, and those few are thought to be sites that developed into tribal capitals. There is no doubt that the bulk of the population lived not in hillforts but in farmsteads scattered across the landscape, some fortified, like **Rispain Camp** in Galloway, and others undefended. Roundhouses were the norm for dwellings, whether built of stone or timber, and they were often associated with stock enclosures and field-systems. Formal burial in built grave-structures was relatively rare during this period, restricted perhaps to the upper classes of society. Evidence of ceremonial places is even more rare. What is known of Celtic society from Roman authors and early folk-tales reveals an emphasis on forest glades, water and boggy places, a reflection of the effect that the wetter climate had wrought on people's lives, and chance discoveries of votive deposits in lochs and bogs bear out the written evidence. Valuable items of bronze and iron were 'buried' in this way, to placate the gods, and it is likely that perishable offerings were also made.

A wide variety of monuments is described in the chapters that follow; each chapter pursues a theme through 4000 years — houses, tombs, ceremonial monuments, and fortifications — so as to show how these aspects of society developed and intermingled. Scotland has a richness in its visible prehistory that may come as both a surprise and a delight.

Seascape with broch: the close relationship between many brochs and the sea is underlined at **Midhowe** on Rousay, Orkney, a reminder of maritime skills.

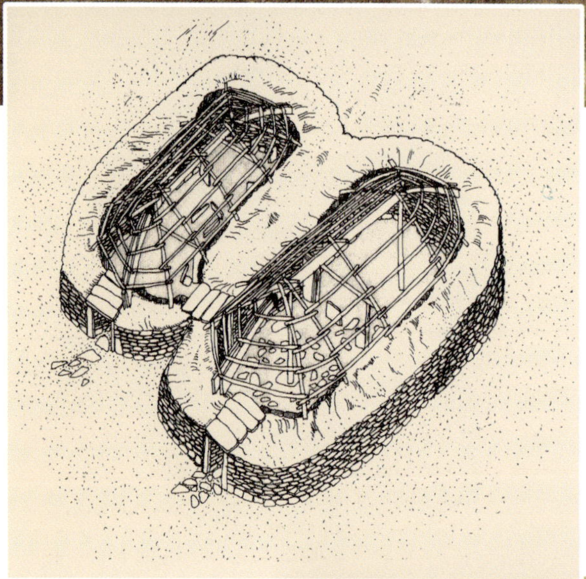

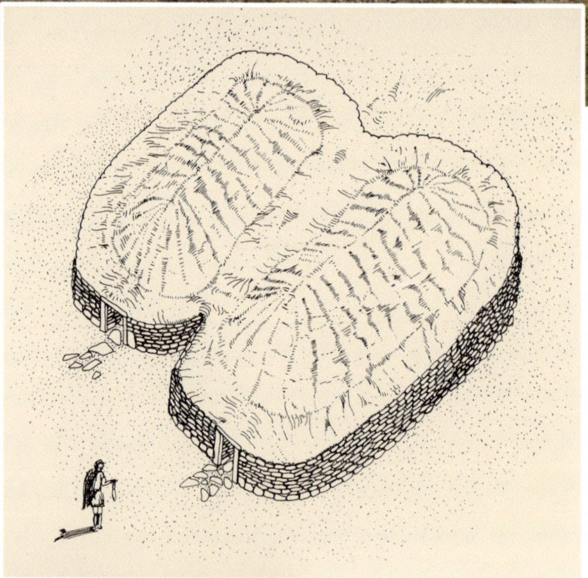

Knap of Howar, Orkney

Top
The houses are still embedded in the sand that once covered them. The spacious dwelling is divided by stone slabs into kitchen and living-room, and the entrance would originally have had a wooden door.

Right
The inner room of the workshop had cupboards and shelves for storing the farm's produce and equipment.

HOUSES OF THE LIVING

Knap of Howar
The great quern, worn by years of grinding grain into flour and shells into rough grit to strengthen the potter's clay, is still in position on the kitchen floor.

IT is perhaps easier to come close to prehistoric people through their houses than by trying to appreciate other forms of their architecture. The house fulfils a basic range of needs: shelter, warmth, a place to cook, eat and sleep, needs as vital now as they were a few thousand years ago. The houses that survive tend to be the successful designs, the dwellings that were inhabited by successive generations, renovated as necessary but showing a familiar human continuity. Less obvious and less familiar are the beliefs that may have ruled the building of a house in early times: why was a tiny, crudely made pot placed in a small pit beside the hearth at **Knap of Howar** in Orkney carefully covered over and hidden? Was the arc of deer jawbones surrounding the hearth of a house on South Uist simply the equivalent of a laird's trophy wall of antlered heads or did it hold some magic potency?

The earliest houses still standing and visible in Scotland are the two at **Knap of Howar** on the Orcadian island of Papa Westray. They have been in state care since 1937, but their identification as neolithic structures came about in 1973 when a decision was taken to undertake archaeological investigation in advance of necessary structural consolidation. There are two oblong houses standing side by side and linked by an interconnecting passage through their adjoining walls. They represent a neolithic farmstead dated by radiocarbon analysis to the later 4th millenium BC, between about 3600 and 3100 BC. Orkney at that time may have consisted of larger land masses and fewer islands than it does today: certainly there is evidence to show that originally **Knap of Howar** lay inland behind sand-dunes, unlike its foreshore location today, and that Papa Westray may have been linked to Westray instead of being a separate island.

The two houses represent a late phase in the history of the farmstead, because they are embedded in an earlier midden, but both the houses and the earlier midden belong broadly to the same phase of neolithic settlement: characterised by mixed farming (barley, cattle, sheep, pigs) and by a special type of decorated pottery known as Unstan Ware. The visible buildings consist of a dwelling house, divided internally into two rooms, and a workshop-cum-barn, divided into three compartments. The internal fittings were created both of stone and of wood: stone was used for room partitions, benches, hearths and cupboards, while wood was also used for benches and for pillars to help support the roof.

Knap of Howar seems to have been a flourishing farm, and the substantially-built farmhouse is in keeping with a successful enterprise, self-supporting in every respect. Aside from the products of animal breeding and cultivation, the inhabitants' diet was supplemented by oysters and other shellfish and by fish, including large cod and other deepsea fish which must have been caught from boats some 3 to 8 km out to sea. Pottery and tools of bone and stone were all made on the farm and nothing had to be imported from outside the island.

There was clearly a link in early times between the designs of houses and tombs, the one the houses of the living and the other the houses of the dead: their architecture being the link between two worlds. The way in which both came to an end was also important. Evidence is accumulating from recent excavations in Orkney to show that, when a house or a tomb was finally abandoned, considerable care might be taken in filling it with layers of selected material (this filling process explains why traces of the original roof are often entirely lacking, because it was removed at the time). These layers can consist of earth, stones, or sand, spiced with shells, or deer antlers, or even human bones, but they represent deliberate, ritual acts. With hindsight, this interpretation may explain the layers of filling that Professor Gordon Childe found in some of the houses at **Skara Brae**: evidence not of later squatters but of sealing houses that could not be used again.

Knap of Howar
Few traces of the original roof were found, but the reconstruction drawings opposite show the most likely method of roofing. The entrance passages are roofed with horizontal stone slabs, and the inner face of the house wall converges inwards at eaves level to reduce the span. The main roof is timber-framed, the ridge beam supported in the case of the dwelling house by two axial pillars, and the outer ends of the rafters resting on the inner wall-head (as in later blackhouses).

SKARA BRAE

Skara Brae, Orkney.

Skara Brae must be one of the best-known prehistoric monuments in Britain. Rightly so, because its astounding state of preservation makes it an extraordinarily evocative glimpse of times long past: some of the houses stand to eaves level, whole stretches of passage-way are still roofed, and much of the stone-built furniture is still in place. This was a small village of some six to eight houses, which were built, modified and rebuilt over a period of some 600 years, between about 3100 and 2500 BC. Its exposed situation today, on the shore of the Bay of Skaill, is the result of marine erosion and is very different from its original setting: it lay in fertile grasslands well back from the sea, an ideal environment for agriculture, animal breeding, fishing and hunting.

Most of the houses display a remarkable uniformity of design, and the best-preserved (which are also the last to have been built) stand fully 3 m high to roof level. Essentially, each house consists of a single squarish room, up to 6.4 m across, within 2 m thick walls, with rounded corners and small cells and cupboards built

The main passage through the village.

within the thickness of the walls. A single doorway has bar-holes to secure a wooden door; opposite the door is a shelved dresser, built of stone, on which the flat-based Grooved Ware pots might have stood (sherds of both plain and elaborately decorated pots were found, some up to 600 mm in diameter). In the centre of the room is a large slab-lined hearth, square or rectangular, sometimes with stone seats alongside, and on either side a stone-panelled bed lies against the wall. The front corner-posts of the beds seem to have been quite tall and may well have supported skin canopies over the beds—of course, there would have been 'mattresses' of heather or straw and luxuriant furs for blankets. Stone tanks set into the floor, their corners sealed with clay, could have held water and perhaps live shellfish softening for bait ready for the next fishing trip—these have been dubbed 'limpet boxes'.

The earlier houses tended to be smaller and to have the beds set into alcoves in the wall, but otherwise the same basic design of house seems to have remained popular over several centuries.

Dresser in House 7.

House 9, one of the earlier houses.

House 1.

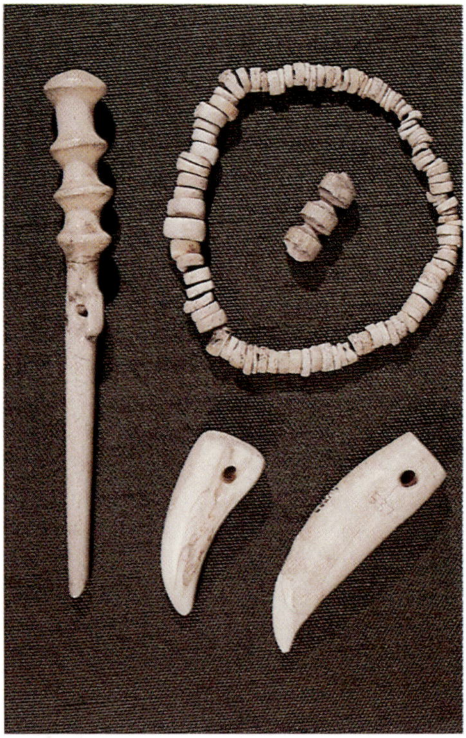

Right
A necklace of bone beads encircling a piece of bone shaped ready to cut into three beads, two tusk pendants and an elaborately carved dress pin.

Far Right
Hard rocks of volcanic origin were used by neolithic people to create prestige items such as maceheads, carved stone balls, and an object from **Skara Brae** (top right) that involved such effort in its making that Professor Gordon Childe described it as 'one of the most astounding monuments of human skill and patience'.

The objects found at Skara Brae underline its status as a domestic settlement of farmers, but some point beyond the immediate to matters of prestige and ritual. The abundant pottery has been mentioned already; there are also tools of flint, stone and bone to help everyday life: axes, mattocks, knives, scrapers for cleaning skins, sturdy bone pins to fasten cloaks of fur. There are items of personal adornment, such as bone beads and pendants, and small containers for red ochre that may have been used for painting on the human body as well as on carved stones. For although the *corpus* of formal neolithic carving in Scotland is small, some relatively informal designs, including linear and dot motifs, have been found on building slabs at Skara Brae.

An area of wet midden yielded finds made of wood and other organic materials that normally decay into nothing: for example, a wooden handle, carefully shaped, and fragments of rope made of heather.

Although the Grooved Ware vessels link Skara Brae with a world that stretched to the south coast of England, there was nothing that could not have been made on the spot by the inhabitants of the village—including some very special stone objects that must be ceremonial rather than functional: a carved stone ball and some strangely knobbed and spiked artefacts, the manufacture of which must have involved considerable effort.

The formal layout of most of the intact and visible houses contrasts with the free-standing building, House 8, on the western edge of the village. Although it shares some features with the other houses (central slab-lined hearth, entrance bar-holes, intramural cell and cupboards), the overall layout of this building is irregular, even before the porch was added to its southern entrance, and it lacks beds, 'limpet boxes' and dresser. It has been variously interpreted as a communal kitchen and industrial workshop—certainly the debris of flint-working was found scattered over the floor. During excavations in the 1970s remains were found of similarly 'irregular' buildings, constructed and later demolished, and used perhaps as outhouses and workshops. If the interpretation of **Knap of Howar** as dwelling house and workshop is correct, a corresponding range of buildings might be expected elsewhere.

Though not in state care and invisible below ground, villages contemporary with and similar to Skara Brae have been discovered and partly excavated at Rinyo on Rousay, at Barnhouse adjacent to the **Stones of Stenness** on Mainland Orkney, at Pool on Sanday and at Noltland on Westray. The houses at Rinyo were particularly close in design to the dwellings of Skara Brae.

Shetland houses

The oval shape and internal alcoves of **Skara Brae** House 8 are reminiscent of neolithic houses in Shetland. Apart from the earliest houses at **Jarlshof,** the only neolithic house in state care there is the atypical hall at **Stanydale,** but the low foundations of many ordinary neolithic and bronze age houses can be seen on the rough moorlands of Shetland, including the area round **Stanydale** itself. A typical house is oval with a thick stone wall, set on a hillslope with the doorway on the downslope side and sometimes with a porch protecting the doorway. Inside there is a single oval room, with alcoves and cells set into the wall. The great hall of **Stanydale** is considerably bigger than other houses and it may well have served a special purpose, perhaps as a tribal assembly-house or as a chieftain's hall. Its interior has an impressive symmetry and the curved megalithic façade either side of the entrance relates its external design to that of contemporary neolithic tombs in Shetland. Two massive post-holes on the internal axis of the hall suggest that it was crowned by a ridged roof of turf or thatch on a wooden frame; during excavation, fragments of spruce were found in one of the post-holes, best explained as driftwood carried by the sea from North America to the shores of Shetland and a welcome gift in a land of meagre wood.

One of the neolithic houses near the **Stanydale** hall.

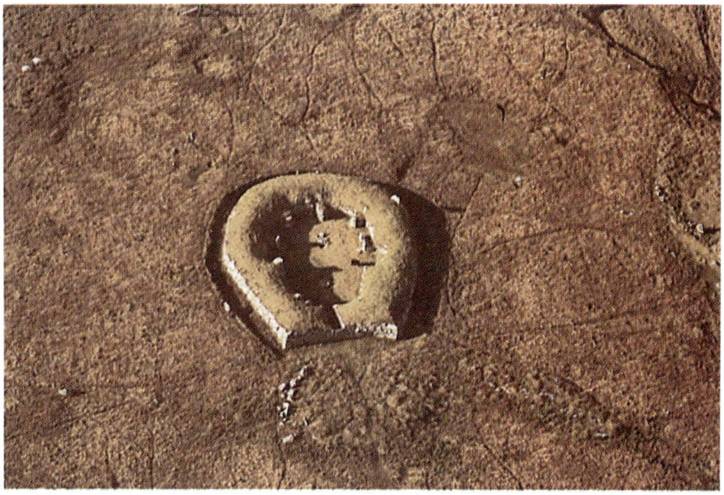

The great neolithic hall at **Stanydale**.

House 8 at **Skara Brae**.

Although apparently isolated, the **Stanydale** hall has several normal houses, field-walls and clearance cairns in its vicinity, and it is this sense of an integrated ancient landscape that make the visible prehistory of Shetland very exciting. Excavation of a complex of houses, enclosures, cairns of stones cleared from fields and a burial cairn at Scord of Brouster, near Walls, has shown that the colonisation of Shetland took place as early as that of Orkney in the 4th millennium BC, and that, even so far north, cereal cultivation was part of the neolithic economy.

JARLSHOF

Jarlshof from the air.

Jarlshof is a truly extraordinary place. To walk round it is to pass through 4000 years, the tangle of walls taking you from the laird's house of the early years of the 17th century AD through medieval and Viking times into prehistory. What better proof could one have of the early farmers' ability to choose prime land than here, where so many later generations maintained that first choice made around 2400 BC? Jarlshof lies at the southern tip of Shetland, beside the shallow bay known as the West Voe of Sumburgh and on the lower slope of the sandstone promontory of Sumburgh Head: an ideal combination of sheltered fishing, a good landing place for boats,

The laird's house.

and fertile, well-drained land with fresh-water springs, while the beach provided an inexhaustible source of good quality building stone.

The laird's house, to which Sir Walter Scott gave the name Jarlshof, was built on top of an artificial mound, the accumulation of earlier centuries. Fierce storms at the end of the 19th century first exposed the iron age buildings below and to the seaward side of the house, and archaeological excavations both then and in the 1930s and 1950s revealed the extensive buildings visible today. Impressive though they are, it is worth remembering that more prehistoric buildings are likely to lie beneath the laird's house and the medieval farmstead and that coastal erosion has destroyed a large part of the prehistoric complex.

Nevertheless, an excellent sequence of prehistoric domestic buildings survives. The earliest building appears to have been oval, the base of its wall simply a stone revetment against the sand in which the house was sunk. Its remains are scanty but they include two intriguing features: a stone-lined pit in the floor in which parts of a human skull, three stone clubs and a stone knife were found, and a smaller pit which contained the four feet of a cow. The bone and stone tools associated with this oval building are broadly similar to finds from **Skara Brae**, and they suggest that neolithic farmers may have settled at **Jarlshof** by about 2400 BC.

Reminiscent of **Skara Brae** is the large stone-kerbed hearth in one of at least four houses that were built later, a little to the seaward side of the first. The design of these houses is easier to understand: they were substantial, free-standing dwellings with thick walls, oval in shape from the outside but inside planned as a series of small cells round a central living area. Small cells were paved and may have been used for storage, while others could have acted as bed-alcoves. These must have been snug, weatherproof houses, probably roofed with turf on a driftwood frame. In two of them the great quern-stones still lie where they were found, their hollows rubbed smooth by the incessant labour of grinding barley for bread and gruel. The design of these houses is typical of Shetland houses of the 2nd and early 3rd millennia BC.

Prehistoric houses.

Steatite workings beside the Catpund Burn at Cunningsburgh, used from prehistoric to medieval times.

This small farming community bred sheep, cattle and a few pigs and grew barley. Tools were made locally of sandstone, slate, steatite, quartz and bone. The soft steatite was also carved into vessels to supplement those made of pottery. Worked outcrops of steatite can be seen beside the Catpund Burn at Cunningsburgh, some 24 km north of Jarlshof.

One of the houses (no III) was later used as a bronzesmith's workshop, after its domestic life was over. To judge by the style of the bronze tools and weapons made here, this happened around 800 BC. Little is visible today of the houses of the wealthy community for which these prestigious bronze items were made; one lay beneath the adjacent roundhouse and others may lie beneath the laird's house.

The next stage in the building sequence shows the same change to roundhouses that was happening in contemporary Orkney. The remains of three such houses are visible in front of the museum; they consist of one large room, up to 7 m across, sometimes with radial divisions creating separate work or storage compartments against the house wall. Two have additional underground storage in the form of a small earth-house, opening from within the wall of the house. The one over which the path crosses in front of the museum has a chamber 3.3 m long and 1.4 m wide, roofed by flat slabs at a height of 1 m—accessible only on hands and knees. Fetching the butter was perhaps a child's task!

Something prodded the iron age inhabitants of **Jarlshof** into a new building enterprise towards the end of the 1st millennium. The precise date is unknown. The reason is also unknown—a need for defence, a desire to display power and prestige, perhaps a combination of such factors? But the result is certain: a broch was built. Only half of it survives, for the sea has destroyed the rest, but it still gives a fine impression of former strength. Its base was solid stone, 5 m thick, round a central court 9 m across, and parts of two intramural cells are visible.

The broch itself conforms to the usual pattern, but a unique feature is the high and strongly built wall that runs from the north side of the broch, apparently enclosing an outer courtyard on the west side. Within the courtyard, fitted snugly in the angle between the broch and courtyard walls, a roundhouse was built, though its plan is now obscured by later buildings. It has free-standing masonry piers that helped both to support the roof and to divide up the interior into convenient paved compartments. This aisled roundhouse may well have been contemporary with the broch.

In time, perhaps around AD 200, the broch and its courtyard were abandoned in favour of newly-built wheelhouses (see page 23), first one large wheelhouse in the old courtyard, then two smaller wheelhouses, one beside the large wheelhouse and the other built inside the old broch. They seem to mark a return to a non-defensive farming life which was to continue into historical Pictish times.

Entrance passage into one of the wheelhouses at **Jarlshof.**

Wheelhouses inside the broch courtyard at **Jarlshof.**

Steinacleit on Lewis is a classic example of archaeological remains so enigmatic that they can be interpreted either as a burial cairn and stone setting or as a domestic house and enclosure. Without excavation, its interpretation remains arguable but a domestic function seems more likely now in the light of excavations elsewhere. Early this century the site was stripped of a metre-thick covering of peat, revealing a large circular structure to which is attached an oval walled enclosure—an animal pen, perhaps, or a working yard. Both the house and the enclosure are similar to the neolithic settlements of Shetland—the house is comparable in size to the great hall of **Stanydale**—and the location of **Steinacleit** is typical of the well-drained hillslope situations of the Shetland farms. Excavations amongst the sand-dunes of Harris, North Uist and Benbecula have uncovered the remains of less substantially-built settlements of the 3rd and 2nd millennia BC whose inhabitants farms the easily cultivated coastal fringe, but **Steinacleit** and the island-settlement in Loch Olabhat, in North Uist, represent the taming of a harsher upland environment.

The same combination of massively-built roundhouse and walled enclosure occurs at **Kilpatrick** on Arran, although the enclosure there is on a larger scale, enclosing almost a hectare within a substantial bank of earth and stone. **Steinacleit** lies close to a loch, whereas **Kilpatrick** borders a small burn running down to the sea. Neither date nor function can be identified as yet. There are traces of relatively recent rig-and-furrow cultivation of the land inside the enclosure, but the enclosure-wall is likely to be considerably earlier. The house entrance opens into the enclosure, and two cells are visible within the thick house-wall. A cist containing a bronze age pot was found within the house-wall, and this, together with the enormous slabs of stone used in its construction, suggests an early prehistoric date.

The roundhouse, whether built of stone or timber, remained the basic form of domestic dwelling throughout most of Scotland down to the early centuries AD. The crannogs of central

Aerial view of the **Steinacleit** homestead, Lewis.

and western Scotland are essentially timber roundhouses built on artificial islands in lochs, and the uplands are speckled with hut-circles (low stone foundations) and hut-platforms (levelled circular platforms on which timber houses could be built on hillslopes). Hillforts could contain whole villages of roundhouses—the fort on Eildon Hill North near Melrose in the Borders encloses several hundred house-foundations—and some of the tiny duns perched on rock-stacks in western Scotland are in effect fortified houses, their precise shape dictated by their rocky base.

The dividing line between village and fort, farm and stronghold, is not always very clear, particularly in the late 1st millennium BC when Celtic society was influenced as much by considerations of honour and prestige as by the dictates of necessity. **Rispain Camp** in Wigtown is best described as a fortified stronghold and therefore is included in the chapter on fortifications (see page 64), but this should not disguise its essential way of life as a farm. Moreover, the character of a settlement can change as the need for defence passes. This is particularly true of brochs, which appear to have been a relatively short-lived and specialised form of defensive structure, often becoming undefended villages as at **Gurness** in Orkney and **Edin's Hall** in Berwickshire.

Earth-houses

Despite their name, earth-houses were not dwellings but cellars, built partially or wholly underground and alongside or attached to houses above ground. They are also known by their French name, *souterrain*, because they are a widespread type of building, found in Brittany, Cornwall and Ireland, as well as in Scotland, but their design, function and date vary from place to place. Even within Scotland there are regional groups, ranging from the massive earth-houses of Angus and Perthshire, averaging some 46 square metres in area and roofed at ground level, to the underground chambers of the Northern Isles that provided a bare 5 square metres of floor space. To judge by the little dating evidence that exists, the smaller northern earth-houses appear to represent a tradition that began some 500 years earlier than those in eastern and southern Scotland, where most seem to belong to the 1st and 2nd centuries AD.

One thing is certain: earth-houses belong to a purely domestic, unfortified context of farming communities. They are not found in hillforts or associated with brochs and duns. The earth-house contrived in the ditch between two ramparts at the fort of **Castlelaw** near Edinburgh belongs to a period when the defensive character of the place was no longer important, its location being an ingenious way of reducing the effort of digging down to make it subterranean.

On mainland Scotland, earth-houses usually take the form of curving, banana-shaped passages, and unexcavated examples show up on aerial photographs as very distinctive crop-marks. In recent years, aerial survey has discovered some 100 earth-houses in Angus, each of which originally must have been part of a farm or a village. Three of the best examples are in state care at **Tealing**, **Carlungie** and **Ardestie**, the first discovered more than a 100 years ago and the other two in 1949 and subsequently excavated. Traces of the houses and workshops to which they belonged were uncovered at **Carlungie** and **Ardestie**, in both cases built of stone like the earth-houses themselves. The structure of such earth-houses is in essence a stone-lined trench sunk into the ground, its level floor carefully paved; the roof seems to have been at ground level and to have consisted either of large stone slabs laid horizontally across the trench or of a timber frame bearing turf or thatch. The reconstruction drawing of Newmill in Perthshire shows the *souterrain* roofed with timber, like the impressive timber roundhouse that it served, covered with earth and turf. A ridged roof has been suggested,

Right
An earth house was built in the ditch of the earlier hillfort at **Castlelaw.** The stone-lined passage follows the curve of the ditch, and two large upright stones mark the entrance into a spacious circular room (the roofing throughout is modern). The earth-house was used in the second century AD, and its owners had acquired Roman pottery and glass.

Far Right
The earth-house at **Tealing** is now open to the air but is likely originally to have had a timber-framed roof at ground level. The stone lining has a basal course of large boulders.

Tealing, Angus
A wooden door could be closed against the stone jambs and sill at the entrance, and a magnificent cup-and-ring marked stone was re-used at the base of the wall.

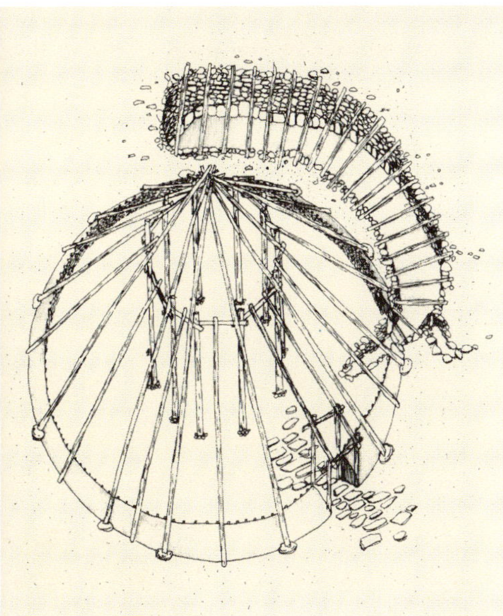

Far Left
Reconstruction of a timber round house and earth-house excavated at Newmill in Perthshire and no longer visible. The earth-house, entered both from within the house and from just outside, was lined with stones and may have had a flat roof carried on wooden beams.

Left
From the outside, the earth-house appeared little more than a bump in the ground, although its presence would have been obvious. The house was thatched over a wooden framework and had an entrance porch.

but a flat roof as shown in the drawing would have been easier to build, just as effective — and could be walked over!

The storage capacity of earth-houses such as these was considerable. No evidence has been found to show what was stored in them, but their cool, dry conditions would be suitable for grain and other foodstuffs. Their size suggests that they served the needs of more than a single family. Indeed, as they coincide in date and location with the Roman occupation of southern and central Scotland in the 1st and 2nd centuries AD, they may even have been used to store grain destined for the Roman army. Excavation has demonstrated that most were filled in deliberately around the turn of the 2nd century, as if they were no longer needed.

Carlungie, Angus
The earth-house at Carlungie is unusually long and complicated with side-passages, although in places its walls survive only at a very low level. Excavation revealed a number of small, round stone houses enclosed within the curve of the earth-house passage.

Ardestie, Angus
At **Ardestie** can be seen not only the lower courses of the earth-house, here furnished with a stone-lined drain, but also (on the left) the remains of contemporary buildings at ground level. These may have been unroofed, paved workshops rather than houses, but there was certainly access at one end directly into the earth-house.

Further north, the pattern begins to change. Earth-houses such as **Culsh** (Aberdeenshire) are smaller and more truly subterranean than those of Angus, though still impressive, and the earth-houses of the far north are smaller still, each the private larder of individual families living in stone-built roundhouses. In the Northern Isles, even the design is different, in that there is a narrow passage leading to a round or oval chamber. In Orkney the chamber is often well below ground level: almost 2 m in the case of **Grain** near Kirkwall. Additional support for the roof is provided by vertical stone pillars in the chamber. Sometimes access to the chamber is so restricted and difficult that a more sinister function than mere storage seems logical. At **Rennibister** in Orkney the passage is only 600 mm wide and 700 mm high, running for 3.5 m before reaching the chamber, and it may not be pure coincidence that a tumbled pile of human bones was found in the chamber (analysis showed that the bones belonged to six adults and about twelve children).

The **Rennibister** chamber is also unusually elaborate, with shelved alcoves set into the walls. One of two earth-houses at **Jarlshof** on Shetland, dating to the mid 1st millennium BC, has a low passage, fully 6 m long, leading to a tiny chamber only about 1.5 m in all dimensions, and it seems most unlikely that this was designed for domestic storage. Access into earth-houses was normally just inside the wall of the house above, as at **Jarlshof** in Shetland. Traces of the ground-level settlement were found at **Grain** in Orkney, together with a second earth-house a few metres away, but these are no longer visible.

Rennibister earth-house showing the entrance passage opening above the level of the chamber floor.

Culsh, Kincardine and Deeside
The boulder-built walls of this earth-house have been stabilised in modern times with concrete; note the massive slabs used as lintels to roof the curving passage. Like those further south in Angus, the whole structure was deliberately filled in with earth when it went out of use.

Grain earth-house near Kirkwall in Orkney.

Looking down from roof level into one of the smaller wheelhouses at **Jarlshof.**

Wheelhouses

The roofs of large roundhouses needed internal support in the form of posts, and these were sometimes also used as a convenient framework for radial divisions within the house, made of wattling or perhaps skin or textile hangings. In the far west and north of Scotland, from the 3rd century AD onwards, there developed an ingenious way of achieving the same result in stone, as an answer probably to the shortage of good timber. This was the wheelhouse: a roundhouse with internal piers of stone, radiating like the spokes of a wheel, that served both to support the roof and to divide up the floor space into compartments surrounding the central hearth. The best-preserved wheelhouses are to be seen at **Jarlshof** in Shetland, but excellent examples have also been excavated in the Western Isles — for some reason, this type of building does not appear to have been popular either in Orkney or on the northern mainland of Scotland.

Wideford Hill, Orkney

The stepped appearance of the cairn today results from robbing of its stones, but the steps betray the internal, concentric wall-faces that gave the finished cairn its stability. The mound is thought to have had a capping of clay originally. The outer part of the passage may always have been open to the sky, but the rest is roofed at a height of only 600 mm.

Superbly sited with a wide view over the Bay of Firth and the islands beyond, **Wideford Hill** is one of a local group of **Maes Howe**-type tombs that includes **Cuween Hill** and Quanterness.

HOUSES OF THE DEAD: BURIAL MONUMENTS

TOMBS for the ancestors played a dominant role in the life of early farming communities. Built to endure the centuries, neolithic tombs are one of the most numerous types of monument in the archaeological record and, to judge by those that have been excavated in modern times, some at least remained in use over very long periods of a thousand years or so. Our best change to appreciate the relationship between life and death, things temporal and spiritual, lies in Orkney, and there it is clear that tombs were built as houses for the dead, their design echoing that of the houses inhabited by the living. Compare the houses at **Knap of Howar,** oblong spaces divided into rooms by slab partitions, with the tombs known as stalled cairns, in which an oblong burial chamber is divided into compartments by slab partitions. The houses at **Skara Brae** consist of a square room with cells opening off it, just as the tomb of **Maes Howe** has a square burial chamber with side cells.

The tombs in state care are all stone-built chambered tombs, but there were also timber and earth versions, where a relatively short-lived chamber built of wood and stone was finally sealed by a covering earthen or stone mound. Excavation of such a timber structure at Lochhill in Galloway showed that it had been replaced by a stone chamber, and it is possible that a similar sequence may lie hidden beneath other stone chambered tombs.

It is estimated that some 500 stone-built chambered tombs have survived in Scotland in various states of preservation. Few are intact, either because of 19th-century antiquarian enthusiasm (it was easier to break in through the roof than to find the entrance) or because they were dismantled at the time when they went out of use — or simply because they were handy sources of stone to build field-walls.

Wideford Hill
In typical fashion, a low opening gives access to one of three side-cells. The level floors of the cells and the main chamber were achieved by cutting into the natural rock of the hillside.

PAGE 26

Pierowall, Orkney
Now in The Orkney Museum in Kirkwall, this magnificent stone once graced a chambered tomb, but the tomb was later dismantled and the carving was only found in 1981. The designs are comparable to the elaborate rock-art of Argyll, as well as to the astounding art of Irish chambered tombs in the Boyne Valley.

The earliest tombs were built around 4000 BC, but the tradition of building and using chambered tombs lasted until at least 2000 BC, and was a tradition common to western Britain, Ireland, and the Atlantic seaboard of Europe. But within the overall tradition were many local differences: each region had its preferred architectural designs as well as its own ceremonial customs, all of which altered and developed as time went on. For the essence of the chambered tomb was that it could be used again and again, its entrance sealed between funerals. This means that an archaeologist excavating a tomb can only try to reconstruct a general picture of the tomb in its final state: as a crude example, if there are the remains of nine individuals in the tomb, that is no guarantee that at an earlier stage in its use there were not 20 more people whose bones were subsequently cleared out.

Despite the uncertainties, the picture that has emerged of how tombs were used is both intriguing and complex. The tombs themselves range from quite simple building enterprises, well within the capabilities of a small community, to sophisticated architectural achievements involving considerable physical effort. The burials seem to represent all ages and both sexes, but the numbers of identifiable individuals vary so much that it is impossible to be certain whether the whole population or selected people were given formal burial in tombs.

Recent work on the bones from a stalled cairn at Isbister on South Ronaldsay in Orkney identified no fewer than 342 individuals, most of whom were represented only by a few bones. Such a high figure for burials in one tomb is unusual, but the partial nature of the skeletons is normal. One explanation has been mentioned already: tombs may have been cleared out periodically or bones taken elsewhere for some reason. Another possibility is that the corpses had been stored elsewhere until the bones were bare and only selected bones taken into the tomb; this practice, known as excarnation, was discovered at Quanterness, another Orcadian tomb, where the bones were bleached and broken. The evidence of age amongst the bones at both Isbister and Quanterness indicates that very few people lived beyond the age of about 25 years — an appalling statistic that has important implications for the handing on of knowledge from generation to generation. The few people who lived as long as 50 years would have had a vital role in maintaining traditions and expertise. Many factors were probably involved in this early mortality rate, but one of them was certainly osteoarthritis, the effects of which are visible on the bones.

Human bones in the main chamber at Isbister, Orkney.

Complete skeletons are not unknown, however, the best evidence coming again from Orkney, from **Midhowe** on Rousay : a very long stalled chamber with 12 compartments, in some of which corpses had been laid on or below stone shelves, their backs to the wall and their knees drawn up to their chests. Nine skeletons were complete, and there were the partial remains of sixteen other people, in all seventeen adults, six adolescents and two children — the tomb was by no means full. For some reason, the burials were confined to the east side of the chamber (apart from one small deposit of bones on the west side), which meant that they were facing west (sunset?).

Although pottery vessels, normally broken, and flint tools are often found amongst the burials, they were not gravegoods in the sense of personal belongings of individuals. The vessels may have played some part in the rituals enacted at the tombs, perhaps including feasting, for bones of domestic animals are also frequent finds. Fragments of at least 30 bowls were found at **Unstan** in Orkney, but that was an unusually rich discovery (this type of pottery, shallow bowls with finely decorated collars, was named Unstan Ware after this tomb). Thus, it was not the individual but the relationship between the living community and the ancestors that was celebrated.

The stalled chamber of **Midhowe**, Orkney.

Unstan, Orkney
Some of the slabs dividing the main chamber into burial compartments have survived as no more than stumps, but this is, nevertheless, a fine example of a stalled cairn. The entrance into a side-cell is visible on the left.

An **Unstan** bowl.

Aside from the bones of domestic animals, there have been a number of cases in which the bones of one particular species have been found in such numbers as to make archaeologists speculate about the presence of some ritual activity other than feasting. Again the examples are from Orkney: on the floor of the burial chamber at **Cuween** were found 24 dog skulls, at Isbister there were the carcases of sea-eagles, and in the small stalled cairn on Holm of Papa Westray North there were deer antlers. In all three cases, the particular species appeared to be specially relevant not only to the use of the tomb but also to its final infilling and closure, and, quite reasonably, the evidence has been interpreted as totemism, signalling the emblem of the community to which the tomb belonged. Others have argued a natural origin, at least for the sea-eagles. The same tomb on Holm of Papa Westray North revealed another interest. In a specially-built stone box, set above floor level, were found the bones of hundreds of small fish — and nothing else, which means that this cannot be dismissed as an otter's lair. Perhaps the fish were a social totem, meaning that this was a tomb of the tribe of the fish, or perhaps they were an offering to ensure that fishing, fundamental to the well-being of the community, was successful.

It is difficult to come close to the ceremonies and beliefs of the communities that built and used chambered tombs, for the archaeological evidence can only act as signposts to possible solutions. Today so many tombs are roofless that one essential factor can pass unnoticed: the hideous difficulty of entering many tombs—dark, foul-smelling and cramped. The passages are often long, narrow and so low that one has to crawl on hands and knees—add to that the smell, the intermittent light from open oil lamps, the burden that had to be dragged. What is so extraordinary about the **Maes Howe**-type of tombs in Orkney is that after this long, degrading, terrifying journey along the passage, one emerged into a burial chamber that soared triumphantly skywards, black and infinite.

The stalled chamber of Holm of Papa Westray North, Orkney.

In western Scotland, the typical chambered tomb, known as the Clyde cairn, was designed as a rectangular chamber built of large slabs set upright; greater height could be achieved by adding drystone walling above the slabs, as at **Nether Largie South** in the **Kilmartin** valley in Argyll (see page 49). **Nether Largie South** also illustrates the ingenious device by which such chambers could safely be lengthened without danger of collapse: the side-slabs overlap one another, and the points of overlap are supported at floor level by cross-slabs to prevent the side-slabs from slipping inwards.

Cuween Hill, Orkney
The round cairn on **Cuween Hill** above the Bay of Firth in Orkney covers an almost intact chambered tomb of the **Maes Howe** type. A long, low passage leads into a rectangular chamber, the walls of which are particularly well-built with thin flagstones, and, although the roof is modern, it is possible to appreciate how the walls gradually oversailed to form a tall chimney-like structure. This photograph shows two of the four entrances into side-cells, each of which had a similarly high corbelled roof.

Holm of Papa Westray North

The fishbones at Holm of Papa Westray North show up as an orange mass within their specially built stone box.

So few tombs still retain their original roofing that it can be difficult to envisage their intact state. For the most part, passages and chambers were roofed by flat slabs or lintels, above which the stones of the cairn could be piled, but the larger round or square chambers were corbelled with overlapping slabs creating a high dome. Given how few people could enter a tomb at any one ceremonial event, the areas outside their entrances were obviously important; in some cases this area was given a focus by a crescentic façade to the tomb itself, and the forecourt thus defined often yields evidence of the dead (**Quoyness, Holm of Papa Westray**), a separation of the dead from the living and yet a close relationship in the landscape as a whole. The superb tomb of **Maes Howe** was surely the resting-place of a great chieftain and appropriately was built in the heart of Orkney close to the great ceremonial complex of the **Brodgar-Stenness** circles.

The Dwarfie Stane, Orkney
Inspired by a gigantic block of sandstone perched on a terrace on Hoy in Orkney, someone had the idea of carving a tomb out of solid rock — the only rock-cut tomb known in Scotland. It could have been the work of a single diligent eccentric (later folklore would have it the home of a famous dwarf).

Cairn O'Get, Caithness
This small but elaborately designed tomb (also known as Garrywhin) is thought to be one of the earliest built in Caithness. Originally the cairn resembled a square with deeply concave sides, at the centre of which lay the burial chamber, now open to the sky (the archaeological term for this type of cairn is short horned).

hearths and other activities, as at **Cairnholy** in Galloway (see pages 32-5).

Most tombs seem to have been located in relation to working farmland, although some were clearly sited with more eye to prestige than convenience, as for example **Carn Ban** on Arran, perched on a hillside some 275 m above sea level. Both on Arran and on Rousay the tombs are spaced in such a way as to suggest the territories of the communities they served. The tomb is often marginal to the best land so as to minimise loss of good agricultural fields or pasture, and in Orkney, where there is a high density of tombs, it is possible to interpret tomb locations in terms of islands of the dead (Calf of Eday) or at least promontories of

Some care was taken to keep the floor level and a block of stone was used to seal the entrance.

Maes Howe, Orkney
The drawing opposite was made in 1861 and shows the many runic inscriptions that were carved in the 12th century AD.

Maes Howe, Orkney

An aerial view of the great tomb shows its overall design. It was built on a rocky knoll amidst a landscape not unlike that of today: a mixture of pasture, arable fields, and open heathland. Around 2700 BC, the knoll was levelled to make a flat surface for the tomb and its mound, and this oval platform was encircled by a wide and shallow ditch, dug to provide earth and clay for the mound. A low stone-based bank was built along the outer edge of the ditch, creating the impression of a tomb set within an earthen circle and underlining its special status.

The main chamber is almost 4.6 m square with a corbelled roof that must originally have reached a height of some 4.5 m above the floor (the concrete dome is modern). Elegantly tapering buttresses in each corner help to support the weight of the roof, one decorated by a series of engraved chevrons (the south-west buttress). The quality of the drystone masonry is superb and some of the stones have been dressed (smoothed to shape); tiny slivers of stone have been inserted to underpin large slabs in the correct position, and advantage was taken of the naturally oblique fracture of the sandstone flags to achieve a smooth yet inwardly curving face to the upper part of the walls.

The entrances to the side-cells, and the three cells themselves, are well above the floor level of the main chamber and could be closed with the blocks of stone that lie before them. Only a few animal bones and a fragment of human skull were found when the tomb was dug out in 1861; the original burials must have been cleared out at some stage.

Cairnholy I,
Dumfries and Galloway
The tomb is at one end of a long cairn of stones, behind a magnificent façade of tall stone pillars. The forecourt was used for ceremonies connected with death and the ancestors.

CAIRNHOLY
Shrines of the Ancestors

On a gently sloping hillside above Kirkdale Glen, overlooking Wigtown Bay, are the two chambered tombs known as **Cairnholy I and II**, the second cairn being only 150 m upslope from the first. Both are open to the sky, for the stones of their covering cairns were robbed long ago to build field-walls, and their dramatic skeletal stones make a jagged outline that was not intended by their builders. They were partially excavated in 1949 by Professor Stuart Piggott and Professor T G E Powell with some unexpected results, not least the evidence for long-distance contacts between Wigtown Bay and the outside megalithic world.

The two tombs are essentially very similar, built to the same basic design, but with important differences: Cairnholy I is more elaborate in every aspect. They may not have been built at exactly the same time but they were certainly in use at the same time for at least part of their long lives as burial places, and it is tempting to see Cairnholy I as the focus for ceremonies, while the second tomb functioned simply as a repository for the dead. Their chambers are very similar but Cairnholy I has a magnificent curving façade of standing stones that forms the backcloth to a forecourt in front of the tomb. Excavation of the forecourt showed that fires had been lit in six

An imaginary reconstruction of a ceremony at the tomb: the forecourt acts as a stage, with the tomb façade as its backdrop and the ordinary people as the audience watching the ritual fires and incantations being performed in honour of the dead.

places at various times, although there was no evidence as to what role the fires had played in the ceremonies. From the charcoal left behind it was possible to identify oak and hazel as fuel for the fires. Beside one of the hearths were found broken pieces of a pottery bowl and a flake of pitchstone from the island of Arran. Beneath another hearth, in line with the entrance to the tomb, was a filled-in pit that the excavators interpreted as the hole in which a single stone pillar had stood during an early stage in the use of the forecourt.

The chambers of both tombs consist of an inner and an outer compartment, with the odd feature that the inner compartment was built as a box, so that it was closed and inaccessible from the oute compartment. It is thought that these box-lik inner chambers were the original tombs an that the outer chambers, and the façade an forecourt of Cairnholy I, were added later. If th original tombs were used more than once, entr must have been via the roof, by lifting th capstone, whereas the outer chambers could b entered between the tall portal stones at thei outer end. Little is known about the burial because acid soil conditions had dissolved all trac of bones apart from a few scraps of burnt an unidentifiable bone. Some of the latest burials i Cairnholy I must have been accompanied by th fragments of a Food Vessel and a stone with a

Cairnholy I

The box-like rear chamber was originally roofed by a great stone slab, resting on the two taller end-slabs and on side-walling now vanished. The roof may have been flush with the top of the cairn so as to allow access to the chamber.

Cairnholy II
Tradition has this as the tomb of Galdus, a mythical Scottish king, perhaps because the tomb has always been such a conspicuous feature in the landscape, perched on a rocky knoll. The two portal stones now lean impossibly close, one broken short and the other strangely pointed.

Below
The inner chamber is still roofed by a single large slab and some of the side-walling survives.

finely carved cup-and-ring mark (six rings) found in the inner chamber and by the late neolithic pottery and flint knife in the outer chamber. The pottery included sherds from a beaker and from a type of decorated bowl normally found in England. An even more exotic find was part of a ceremonial axe made of jadeite, found on the floor of the outer chamber. Jadeite is a beautiful green stone that was imported into Britain from a source in the Alps, and jadeite axes were clearly prestigious objects that reflected the wealth and power of their owners. They are usually encountered in deliberately buried hoards or as isolated finds, rather than as gravegoods, but the Cairnholy discovery is only a small fragment of what was once a magnificent axe.

The final activities at Cairnholy II were also associated with broken beaker pottery, and a fire had been lit in the outer chamber. Both tombs were then sealed. The entrance to the tomb was blocked by placing a tall pillar against the portals, and the sacred forecourt at Cairnholy I was piled with stones, with here and there a small offering of broken pottery, a flake of pitchstone or a few handfuls of shellfish.

On the bleak brown moorlands of Caithness lie the **Grey Cairns of Camster,** two great mounds of pale grey stone amongst the sodden peat. From the Round Cairn in the foreground can be seen the humped profile of the Long Cairn in the distance. The landscape has been altered by tree-planting since these photographs were taken.

The Round Cairn, impressive in itself, is also a useful illustration of what the early stages of the Long Cairn would have been: individual tombs within their own circular cairns.

Inside the **Camster** Round Cairn is a well-preserved burial chamber with large upright slabs dividing it into compartments.

Like the **Cairnholy** tombs, many chambered cairns seem to have undergone a long process of modification, transforming quite simple designs into composite architectural monuments. There are cairns in Caithness in state care where tombs within small round cairns have later been incorporated into immensely long, huge cairns: **Camster Long** cairn and probably **Cnoc Freiceadain**.

Camster Long Cairn
Two separate burial chambers and their covering round cairns have been incorporated into a cairn almost 70 m long with projecting 'horns' forming curved façades at either end. In common with the Round Cairn some 183 m away, the tomb entrances face to the south-east.

Between the paired slabs dividing up the burial chamber can be seen the entrance passage of the southern tomb in **Camster** Long Cairn.

The northern chamber is a simple oval design with its walls carried on a basal course of upright slabs.

One special group of tombs known as Clava cairns seems to span the categories of funerary and non-funerary ritual particularly well. The cairns are encircled by free-standing stone pillars, a combination of tomb and stone circle, and as tombs they seem to have held only one or two burials (because of this it has been suggested that they were family shrines rather than burial places, but, in a sense, all tombs were shrines to the dead). In some cases the cairn covered a regular chamber and entrance passage, whereas in others the cairn formed an unbroken ring round an open space which may eventually have been sealed by a filling of stones—the distinction is now blurred for the visitor because all are open to the sky. At **Clava** itself, near Inverness, there are two chambered cairns (or passage-graves) and a ring-cairn, as well as a small kerb-cairn such as elsewhere is often a component of stone circles (for example **Temple Wood** in Argyll). Indeed the ring-cairn with its encircling standing stones is echoed by the recumbent stone circle at **Loanhead of Daviot** in Aberdeenshire and elsewhere. In many ways the Clava cairns are a reminder to the archaeologist not to categorise the evidence too neatly, particularly as their dating is far from clear.

Later burial cairns of the 2nd millennium BC sometimes have kerbs of massive stones, as at **Auchagallon** and **Moss Farm** on Arran. The cairn at **Moss Farm** has been almost entirely removed in later times to build field-walls, leaving its kerb looking disconcertingly like a stone circle.

Balnuaran of Clava
The central ring-cairn is now reduced almost to its base; three of its nine encircling pillars can be seen beyond, and, on the distant right, one of the passage graves.

The passage and burial chamber of the north-east cairn were originally roofed over, and the intact cairn must have been more than 3 m high.

This cup-marked stone is one of the slabs at the base of the outer wall of the north-east cairn. Another, less-weathered, group of 10 cups may be seen on the basal slab to the immediate left of the entrance into the chamber of the south-west cairn. Many other cup-marked stones were hidden in the walls of chambers.

Corrimony, Glen Urquhart
The cairn is encircled by 11 standing stones, and the entrance-passage is still partly roofed. A large slab decorated with more than 20 cup-marks originally crowned the corbelled roof of the chamber.

Cist Burials

The individual burials with beakers that became fashionable after 2000 BC are often far more splendid in terms of rich gravegoods than the old tomb burials, but they lack the architectural achievement of the tomb-builders. The body was placed, knees drawn up, in a short cist, or stone-built coffin, sometimes under a conspicuous cairn as at **Memsie,** near Fraserburgh, or more often in cemeteries barely marked above ground. These have frequently been found purely by accident during gravel excavation or agricultural activities, and are excavated as rescue operations. Sometimes beaker burials were added to older monuments, perhaps signalling the passing of the old order and the dominance of the new. Such burials were made in the chamber of the tomb of **Nether Largie South** in the Kilmartin glen in Argyll, while at the recumbent stone circle at **Loanhead of Daviot** in Aberdeenshire sherds of broken beakers played a part in the final rituals marking the abandonment of the circle. The flat bronze axe, typical of the products of the early metalworkers, was immortalised by the carvings on three cists in the **Kilmartin** complex.

Burials in cists could also contain a different type of pottery known as Food Vessels; they were in use contemporary with later beakers, and they accompanied both inhumation (unburnt) and cremation burials. By the middle of the 2nd millennium, cremation seems to have become the preferred burial rite, and a variety of pottery urns developed as containers. The complex monument at **Cairnpapple** is an excellent illustration of how funerary customs altered over the centuries.

Memsie, near Fraserburgh
This was once one of a group of three immense cairns, so large and bare of soil that it has never become grass-grown. With a diameter of 24 m and a height over 4m, this is one of the most impressive burial cairns in Scotland, built for some magnate in the early 2nd millennium BC, although it has been suggested that the present cairn is in fact the result of dumping the other two cairns on top of a smaller original cairn.

CAIRNPAPPLE
A Prehistoric Sanctuary

To stand on Cairnpapple Hill in West Lothian on a clear day is to appreciate instantly why this spot was chosen as a sacred place of death. Though not itself specially conspicuous, it possesses a spectacular panorama of Scotland in all directions. A long sequence of ceremonial and burial activities took place on this hill between about 2800 BC and 500 BC.

The sequence began with an arc of small pits, most of which contained token amounts of burnt human bones, one with a small bone dress pin, broken and burnt. This cremation cemetery was later enclosed within the ditch and bank of an oval henge monument (see page 47), with entrances to north and south. A ring of 24 standing stones once existed within the henge,

The Sanctuary on Cairnpapple Hill

Aerial view of **Cairnpapple** cemetery and henge.

and some kind of rectangular stone structure stood at its centre (a similar arrangement to the **Stones of Stenness**).

A burial, perhaps a child (no bones survived but the grave was too small for an adult), with a beaker was placed beside one of the standing stones, and another beaker grave was built inside the circle after the central rectangular setting had been removed. This was a splendid grave with its own standing stone and covering cairn outlined with a boulder kerb. Although its gravegoods were few and included no obviously prestigious metal or imported items, this must have been the grave of

After excavation, the monument was reconstructed: within the bank and ditch of the henge, a stony area edged by large stones marks the extent of a huge round cairn that once covered the smaller mound now rebuilt in its centre. The shallow pits left in the stony area originally held burnt human bone, and the modern steps lead to a hatch by which the visitors may enter the burial mound.

Inside the modern concrete dome may be seen the stones of two graves. Contemporary with the mound is the cist in the foreground, a form of coffin made by lining and roofing a pit with slabs. It contained human bones and a pottery jar known as a Food Vessel, which had originally stood on a small ledge built into one side of the cist. The oval ring of stones beyond was the kerb of a small earlier mound covering a shallow pit, with the tall stone standing like a sentinel at the foot of the grave. Within the pit were found traces of a body, probably lying full length with a round wooden object laid over the head; at the feet had been placed a pottery beaker with a wooden lid, and another beaker stood near the head, both probably containing food or drink. A large wooden club lay alongside the body.

someone important, set within the sacred circle on its hilltop. Its two fine beakers may have held some precious liquid, and the wooden objects—a club, a lid to one of the beakers, and a possible face-mask — may have been intricately carved before they rotted away leaving only their stained and blurred outlines.

The stone pillar at the foot of this grave has remained standing over the subsequent 4000 years. Most, if not all, of the stones of the henge circle were removed when a large cairn was built on top of the earlier beaker grave, but the beaker pillar stood within the blanketing mound—indeed, when Cairnpapple was excavated in the 1940s by Professor Stuart Piggott, the top of the pillar could be seen protruding from the later mound. This new mound had its own kerb of massive boulders, some of which were probably the original standing stones, and was built to house another important burial, this time in a large cist with a Food Vessel. The cairn was later enlarged to a diameter of about 30 m, twice its original size, when two cremated burials in cinerary urns were placed, upside down, in shallow holes.

Beakers from **Cairnpapple,** West Lothian.

Food Vessel from **Cairnpapple.**

Even then, the long history of Cairnpapple was not over. No more major alterations were made to the site, by now simply a massive cairn with traces of the silted-up henge ditch around it, but, after an interval of perhaps a thousand years or more, four long cist graves were dug on the east side of the cairn, between cairn and ditch. Cairnpapple had remained a sacred place. Among the place names listed for this part of Scotland in the Ravenna *Cosmography*, a document compiled in the 7th century AD, is the name *Medio Nemeton*, the Middle Sanctuary. As Professor Piggott speculated in his excavation report, could Cairnpapple have been that Middle Sanctuary, 'whence one looked across Britain at her narrowest, from sea to sea'?

Cemeteries

Recumbent stone circles are described in connection with ceremonial monuments in the next chapter, but they are also strongly associated with death. In some cases there is a low ring-cairn inside the circle, although this may have been an addition to the original layout. A separate cremation cemetery was created beside the circle at **Loanhead of Daviot** in Aberdeenshire: enclosed within two semi-circles of low walling was a number of cremations contained in pottery urns and placed upside down in small pits, some marked by tiny cairns of stones. At the centre of the cemetery was a shallow grave in which a corpse had been cremated; scraps of burnt bone survived to show that the body (a man aged about 40 years) had been laid on its side, facing south, arms outstretched in front of it and apparently holding a stone pendant, and a pyre, mostly willow branches, had been piled on top and fired. There must also have been a layer of highly combustible material beneath the body to have enveloped it in the high temperatures required for cremation. This cemetery takes the dating of the sacred place on to around 1200 BC, at least a thousand years after the stone circle was built. Whatever the rituals for which the circle was designed, the emphasis was ultimately on human burial. Excavation of a recumbent stone circle at Berrybrae near Fraserburgh in Aberdeenshire revealed that the circle had been virtually demolished in order to replace it with a cremation cemetery enclosed within a stone wall, again pointing to a shift in emphasis to funerary rites and burial.

Before the end of the 2nd millennium BC, the custom of formal burial in grave monuments marked and visible above ground level had been abandoned. It may be that the effects of a worsening climate made such reverent displays a luxury ill-fitted to a harsher life. Whatever the reason, burial monuments disappear from the archaeological record over the next thousand or so years. When they reappear in the last few centuries BC, the rite is again inhumation and the burials placed beneath barrows, sometimes surrounded by square ditches and grouped in cemeteries, or placed in stone cists either as individual graves or as multiple graves in which several bodies were interred together. The rite of inhumation was to continue into early Christian times.

Cinerary urn from **Cairnpapple.**

Loanhead of Daviot
The positions of some of the cremation burials are marked by small cairns. The whole cemetery is enclosed within a low wall, with two wide entrances.

The Ring of Brodgar, Orkney

If the stones were regularly spaced, there would have been originally no fewer than 60 in this circle, some of which may have been cut from the 3 m-deep ditch.

CIRCLES AND CEREMONIES

DURING the 3rd and 2nd millennia BC, many stone, timber and earthen monu— ments were created that seem to have had a special ceremonial purpose. They were not built as dwellings, although they may have food debris in them; they were not built as tombs, although there may be traces of death and burial. These are the circles and alignments of standing stones and timber pillars and the earthen henge monuments that belong to the spiritual side of life about which archaeology can prove very little. In the absence of writing to explain them, the material remains left as embodiments of beliefs are frustratingly difficult to interpret—one can speculate, or make informed guesses based on modern ethnography, but such 'answers' may bear little resemblance to ancient reality. It seems reasonable to view these monuments as temples and meeting-places but to admit that we will never have more than a rudimentary idea of what went on there.

The Ring of Brodgar, Orkney
From the air, the stones and their encircling ditch can be appreciated as a perfect double ring; this sacred place became a focus for later burial mounds.

The central circle at **Callanish,** Lewis.

There are some intriguing contrasts. Compare the immense size of the **Ring of Brodgar** in Orkney, with a diameter of about 103 m inside the circle, with the tiny circle at **Callanish** in Lewis. Hundreds of people could have gathered inside the **Ring of Brodgar**, whereas only an élite handful could perform inside **Callanish**, where much of the space is in any case taken up by a burial tomb. It has to be admitted that the interior of **Brodgar** has not been excavated and that there may have been structures of which no surface trace remains, but nevertheless the contrast in size ought to reflect a difference in ceremony. Adjacent to **Brodgar**, excavation inside the **Stones of Stenness**, a circle some 30 m across, produced evidence of sparse structures: in the centre, a square stone setting looking like a giant **Skara Brae** hearth, with four flat slabs outlining a 2 m square, and traces of some kind of timber and stone setting leading from the central setting towards the entrance. Animal bones found in the ditch include cattle and sheep and may have been the debris from feasting or sacrifice, while a human finger-bone may point to ancestor worship rather than human sacrifice or mutilation.

These two monuments, together with the various standing stones and burial mounds clustered round them, are a clear example of a sacred place that became a focus for ceremonial activities over a long period. Other ceremonial centres have been identified at **Callanish** on Lewis, in the **Kilmartin** valley in Argyll, at Balfarg in Fife (where the stone circle of Balbirnie contained a rectangular stone setting as at **Stenness**) and elsewhere. The Orcadian complex can be seen in a wider perspective of contemporary society. With radiocarbon dates showing that it was built soon after 3000 BC, the **Stones of Stenness** circle belongs to the heyday of neolithic affluence, the

The Stones of Stenness, Orkney
Forbidding in their strength after 5000 years, these are the survivors of what was once a circle of 12 tall stones, isolated in its ancient landscape within a massive rock-cut ditch and bank.

society of **Skara Brae** and the great chambered tombs such as nearby **Maes Howe**. Sherds of Grooved Ware vessels found at **Stenness** represent a fashion shared not just at **Skara Brae**, some 10 km away, but also at a settlement adjacent to **Stenness** itself, at Barnhouse. The precise date at which the **Ring of Brodgar** was built is unknown.

Both **Brodgar** and **Stenness** belong to a uniquely British class of site known as henge monuments: earthen rings consisting of a ditch and outer bank (the latter has often been eroded flat over the centuries), within which there may be timber or stone circles. **Stenness** is one of the earliest henges known, a fact that underlines Scotland's place in the mainstream of new ideas, despite the apparent remoteness of places such as the Northern Isles on the fringe of the known world of those times.

The central setting at the **Stones of Stenness,** Orkney.

Standing stones are so familiar a component of the Scottish landscape that it is perhaps difficult to envisage their timber equivalents, yet it is clear from a number of excavations that timber posts were once as much a part of ritual settings as standing stones. There were small wooden structures, perhaps mortuary houses, inside the stone circles at **Loanhead of Daviot** and the **Stones of Stenness**, and a single pole at the centre of the **Stenness** circle echoes the tall stone at the centre of the **Callanish** circle, both perhaps acting like the gnomon of a sundial. One of the stone circles at **Temple Wood** in Argyll replaced an earlier timber circle, and the same replacement of timber by stone has been found at Croft Moraig in Perthshire and at Balfarg in Fife. Only excavation can demonstrate the original presence of timber posts, and it may well be that they were more common than we imagine. Less arduous than stone to set up, a timber circle could be the first stage in the creation of a sacred place, an effort well within the capabilities of a few families.

Many of the stone circles and alignments represent public building on a massive and labour-intensive scale. The stones had to be selected or quarried then dragged on rollers or sledges to the prepared building-site. Holes had to be dug and the stones levered and hauled upright in their sockets, wedged and packed round with stones and earth. In the case of henge monuments, there was the additional work of digging the ditch and creating a bank with the soil and stone dug out. Estimates of the effort involved can only be a rough guide, but building the **Ring of Brodgar**, for instance, with its ditch cut into solid rock, would have taken some 80,000 man-hours. Looked at as a whole, this ceremonial complex in the heart of Orkney represents an enormous investment of time and labour.

The ditch of the **Stenness** henge was dug into solid bedrock.

The Kilmartin Glen

One half of the double spiral
at **Temple Wood.**

THE KILMARTIN GLEN
A Ritual Landscape

The extraordinary concentration of prehistoric activity in the Kilmartin area of Argyll makes this an exciting place to visit. From Kilmartin itself southwards to beyond Cairnbaan on the Crinan Canal, side-roads from the A816 give access to or views of a wide range of ritual and burial monuments, spanning the period from before 3000 BC to about 1200 BC, by which time the growth of peat was well established on the glen floor.

A dominant feature of the glen is the line of burial cairns running southwards from below Kilmartin village. This linear cemetery was developed over more than a thousand years and began not at one end but at the middle with the chambered tomb known as **Nether Largie south.** This was originally a typical Argyll tomb with a long, rectangular chamber divided into four burial compartments by upright slabs set into the floor; it was probably set at one end of a long cairn with an impressive entrance into the chamber, but continued use over the next 1000 years altered the shape of the cairn and obscured the entrance. At least two cist burials were added outside the chamber, and the extra stones covering them created the circular cairn that survives today (one cist can still be seen to the south-west of the chamber; the other, on the north side, contained a Food Vessel).

During the 2nd millennium BC, either side of this early tomb, later burial cairns were built in a line running SSW-NNE: **Ri Cruin**, **Nether Largie Mid**, **Nether Largie North** and the **Glebe Cairn**. These cairns were built for individual burials in cists and some had later burials added. They are outstanding as a group because of the carvings of bronze axes associated with three of the sites. In each case the outline impression of a typical flat axe-head has been pecked into the surface of slabs forming the cist, sometimes accompanying cup-marks: **Nether Largie North** has two axe-carvings on an end-slab and 10 axes and some 40 cup-marks on the underside of the covering slab, **Nether Largie Mid** has one axe and one cup on an end-slab, and **Ri Cruin** has seven axes on an end-slab. Appropriately, as the axe is a wood-working tool, some of the cist-slabs are grooved to fit together like a wooden box (the north cist at **Ri Cruin** is a particularly good example). Further down the glen, **Dunchraigaig** is another cairn of the 2nd millennium BC with two of its burial cists visible.

The burial chamber of **Nether Largie South.**

Nether Largie North Cairn

Below
One of the cists added outside the tomb, **Nether Largie South.**

Below Right
The decorated cist inside **Nether Largie North.**

Axe carvings at Ri Cruin

Visually the most interesting monument and, because of its careful excavation, the best understood is the stone circle complex at **Temple Wood** (the evocative name dates only from the 19th century when peat and stone debris were cleared away and trees planted). There are two circles but only one is intact (South-west Circle). The other (North-east Circle), now traceable by modern concrete markers, was discovered in 1979 during excavation. The latter began as a setting of timber posts, which was replaced before 3000 BC by an elliptical ring of stones; this stone setting appears not to have been completed for some reason, perhaps because the decision had been taken to build another circle alongside. This, the South-west Circle, is in fact oval rather than circular and consisted originally of 22 standing stones, though some were removed in later times. One of the surviving stones is decorated with a double spiral uniquely spread over two of its faces.

Temple Wood Stone Circles

Temple Wood
The central cist inside the south-west circle.

Two small cairns covering cist burials were built just outside the circle, one burial accompanied by a beaker, three flint arrowheads and a flint scraper. Other burials were placed inside the circle but their dating is uncertain: the central cist was covered by a small cairn of which the low kerb is visible as a ring of small upright stones. In its final design, the stone circle was enclosed within a wide bank of stones (this covered over the two external cairns), and the whole, quite complicated, sequence seems to have taken place within the 2nd millenium BC.

Contemporary perhaps with the main circle at **Temple Wood** is a henge monument at Ballymeanoch, now ploughed almost flat; this important site is associated with cist-burials (one accompanied by a beaker), cairns and linear settings of standing stones. Another striking alignment of standing stones in the valley is at Nether Largie, opposite **Temple Wood**.

Highlighting the importance of the Kilmartin area are several oustanding expanses of rock carving: the displays of cup-and-ring marks at **Ballygowan, Baluachraig, Kilmichael Glassary,** Ormaig, **Cairnbaan** and **Achnabreck** are amongst the finest and most elaborate in Scotland (see pages 58-9).

The fort on the rocky hill of **Dunadd** was built in early historic times by the Scots of Dalriada and falls outside the scope of this book.

Achnabreck, Argyll
Several decorated outcrops together form the largest concentration of rock-art in Scotland. Among the many multiple rings are the largest examples yet discovered: up to nine rings and overall diameters approaching a metre.

Achnabreck, Argyll

Geometry and Astronomy

The fact that some stone circles are oval or elliptical rather than truly circular may suggest that their builders had some knowledge of basic geometry. It is easy enough to lay out a circle on the ground by tying one end of a piece of string to an anchor peg and, holding the other end taut, walking round the peg in an exact circle, but the deliberate creation of other figures requires more skill. Professor Alexander Thom argued that the circle-builders must have understood right-angled triangles and how to use them, but such knowledge may be out of keeping with contemporary technology—and one needs only two stakes and a loop of string to create an oval and more stakes for other shapes such as flattened circles.

Tomnaverie
Set in a classic hilltop location, with wide views over the countryside, this recumbent stone circle surrounds a low cairn with a pronounced boulder-kerb.

Loanhead of Daviot
A circle of eight stones, a recumbent slab and two flanking pillars, **Loanhead of Daviot** is one of the best-preserved examples of a tradition special to Aberdeenshire. Most of the interior space is taken up by a low cairn edged with boulders.

Frost has split into two the once majestic recumbent stone.

In recent years there has been similar controversy over megalithic astronomy. Archaeologists agree that the design of many circles and other monuments suggests an interest in the sun and moon rising and setting, but arguments that attempt to interpret these sites as complicated astronomical observatories are sometimes based on faulty evidence—for instance, the stones themselves have fallen and been re-erected in the past and are not now in precisely their original positions. This does not lessen the impact of sites where a deliberate alignment on sun or moon is obvious. The design of the recumbent stone circles of north-east Scotland shows a consistent interest in the rising or setting of the moon in the southern sky: they are built in places where there is an open view to the south, and the recumbent slab with its flanking pillarstones is arranged so as to frame the moon when viewed from inside the circle. The recumbent itself is often a majestic slab requiring special effort to manoeuvre it into place—the largest, at Old Keig in Aberdeenshire, weighs about 61 tonnes (53 tons) and was transported over a distance of some 10 km from its source. Such effort underlines the importance of the circles to the communities that built them, and part of that importance was undoubtedly their association with the moon.

The recumbent stone circle is a highly distinctive variation on the circle theme; it dates to the later 3rd and 2nd millennia BC and is restricted in its distribution to Aberdeenshire, especially the area round Alford. Similar, but later, circles in south-west Ireland seem to indicate influence, if not actual immigration, from north-east Scotland, and there are several related monuments on the route between these two areas (ie down the Great Glen, southwards along the Scottish coast and across the Irish Sea). **Auchagallon** on Arran is a cairn on a terrace above the sea; it has a kerb of large boulders, including a low broad slab flanked by two tall slabs. **Torhousekie** in Wigtown is a stone circle showing the gradation in height of its upright stones that is typical of recumbent stone circles. Inside the circle is a ring-cairn with a setting of three stones resembling a recumbent and flankers. Dr Aubrey Burl has described this monument as an 'idiosyncratic recumbent stone circle', noting that its design seems to be related to the midwinter sunrise rather than to the moon.

At **Callanish** on Lewis there appears to be an interest in the cardinal points: from a circle of stones with a central pillar run lines of stones to north, south, east and west. But the site lies on a ridge with a north-south axis—was this a deliberate choice and are the four alignments more than a desire for symmetry? As elsewhere, the finer points of the design must remain arguable. What is certain is that Callanish is part of a remarkable

Torhousekie, Wigtown
Known also as Torhouse, this is a slightly flattened ring of 19 low stones, graded in height, within which a setting of three stones (a recumbent and two flanking stones) may be the remains of a small ring-cairn. Another setting of three stones lies to the east of the circle on a low crest.

Left
The kerb of the **Auchagallon** cairn, Arran, with its 'recumbent and flankers'.

Callanish from the air.

Cnoc Ceann a' Gharaidh, Lewis

Garynahine, Lewis

Inside the central circle at **Callanish** is a chambered tomb.

ritual landscape and the product of an extensive and flourishing neolithic population. There are several other circles in the vicinity, as well as other settings of stones, and the four major monuments round the north and east sides of Loch Ceann Hulavig appear from their careful siting to have been intended to be intervisible (**Callanish**, **Cnoc Ceann a' Gharaidh**, **Cnoc Fillibhir** and Garynahine, also known respectively as Callanish I-IV).

Our understanding of where the contemporary inhabitants of Lewis lived has been hampered both by the later blanket of peat and by the loss of the contemporary coastline owing to rising sea level and erosion; current work is nevertheless producing evidence of both coastal and inland settlement. Excavation at **Callanish** itself has demonstrated that the tiny chambered cairn inside the circle was part of the original design, rather than a later addition, and both date from around 3000 BC. In its design, the tomb has more in common with Orkney tombs than with local Hebridean examples, and links between the two areas are also apparent in contemporary tastes in decorated pottery.

Machrie Moor, Arran

Callanish takes pride of place among stone circles for the brilliant concept of its design and for affinity with its landscape, but there are other settings with equally compelling qualities. The stone rows of Caithness and Sutherland consist of some of the smallest standing stones yet they have a stunning visual impact through their numbers and overall design: the aptly named **Hill o'Many Stanes** at Mid Clyth in Caithness still boasts some 200 stones arranged in 22 rows. If the fan-shaped pattern was complete, there would be about 600 stones in rows running north-south down a south-facing slope. Apart from their setting in the wild heartland of Arran, the circles on **Machrie Moor** are memorable for their contrasts. Some were built of granite boulders, low, squat and grey, while others were built of tall, red sandstone pillars—the one earthfast and the other skyborne. In another circle the builders have alternated granite and limestone, by nature two different shapes and textures. There is also a tantalising sense of a hidden ancient landscape, because the outlines of cairns and hut-circles push through the peat and an entirely unsuspected low stone circle was found recently by excavation—along with traces of wooden fencing outlining plots of land that pre-date the circles.

Far Left
Machrie Moor

Left
Hill O'Many Stanes, Caithness
Individually the stones are insignificant but in their purposefully massed rows they are oddly moving. Are they 'ghost-paths' along which the spirits of the ancestors could be summoned? Or could they be paths for the living, each clan segregated for a formal occasion?

East Aquhorthies, Aberdeenshire
The circle of pinkish stones with two grey sentinels flanking the huge recumbent is set in a low bank (the vertical outer face is modern). There may once have been a central cairn.

Colour can be appreciated as part of the design of other monuments as well as on **Machrie Moor**. At **Auchagallon** cairn on Arran, the kerbstones are all red sandstone except for the 'recumbent' and its opposite number on the far side of the cairn, which are pale grey granite. Amongst recumbent stone circles, **East Aquhorthies** near Inverurie in Aberdeenshire consists of pink porphyry and red jasper, except for the tall flanking pillars of grey granite on either side of a red granite recumbent slab.

Cairnbaan, Argyll
There are some fine examples of multiple rings on one of several decorated rock-surfaces.

Rock Carving

Scotland possesses an astounding richness of prehistoric rock carving, principally concentrated in Argyll. Apart from a few realistic designs, such as the axe, this rock-art takes the form of cup-marks, cup-and-ring marks, spirals, stars, and linear grooving, often densely covering large expanses of natural rock-face. Such displays are difficult to date, but these designs are also found in archaeological contexts such as tombs and it is clear that their potential date-range is very long, from the mid 4th millennium BC to around 1000 BC. Their overall distribution stretches from Galloway to Shetland and they are part of a widespread tradition of rock-art in Britain, Ireland, Brittany, and north-west Spain; the concentration of carvings in Argyll may well reflect the western seaways through

Baluachraig, Argyll
A crisp and unweathered group of carvings.

Drumtroddan, Wigtown

One of several groups of carvings, the natural rock surface is here decorated with cup-marks, cup-and-rings (up to six rings) and grooves. Not far away on this plateau is an alignment of three tall standing stones, one now fallen.

Below

Cullerlie, Aberdeenshire

This is one of the most curious of ancient monuments – small, compact and orderly. It stands on a tongue of gravel that was formerly almost surrounded by bogland, a desolate setting to which all the stones had to be carried or dragged from the higher ground. There is a sense of precise purpose, for within the low circle of eight granite boulders are eight tiny kerb-cairns, each outlined by a necklace of eleven stones – except for one that has only nine. The largest cairn is set at the centre of the circle and has a double kerb. Excavation showed that fire had played a part in the ceremonies of building: once the circle and the eight kerb-rings were in position, willow branches had been laid between them and set on fire. Inside the rings were laid tokens of burnt human bone and charcoal, covered over by stones.

which a familiarity with rock-art spread. Some people have tried to read a symbolism into cup-and-ring marks, but one can only speculate about the original significance of these designs.

Similar carvings are often found on standing stones, both formal settings as at **Temple Wood** in Argyll and **Loanhead of Daviot** in Aberdeenshire, and isolated stones, and thus are often associated with death in the form of burials or token deposits of human bone.

Both cup-marks and cup-and-ring marks have been discovered in later contexts, but they are more likely to be old stones re-used than late examples of carving. One such carved stone was incorporated into the outer wall of the broch at **Midhowe** on Rousay, and a superb example was built into the passage of the earth-house at **Tealing**, near Dundee. Rock carving is, after all, a very satisfying form of art.

The Caterthuns, Angus,
from the air.

STRONGHOLDS HIGH AND LOW

WHEN were Scotland's earliest fortifications built? This is a deceptively simple question—and virtually impossible to answer. Our modern appreciation of what ranks as defences may not match the view of prehistoric people, even if we had a complete record of what they built, and our judgement must depend upon structural traces and discoveries of weapons. On that basis, prehistoric society appears to have been relatively peace-loving until the early part of the 1st millennium BC, with one possible exception: a massively stockaded enclosure built in late neolithic times at Meldon Bridge in the Borders, but even that may have been motivated by prestige rather than defence. Towards the end of the bronze age, however, there are clues to suggest that society was changing and becoming more aggressive. Bronzesmiths began to produce in large quantities items such as swords and shields that can only be weapons and defensive arms rather than equipment for hunting—the bronzesmith working at **Jarlshof** around 800 BC was making swords amongst other things. At the same time, the first defensive forts were being built. Some of the earliest forts were those built with stone walls laced with timbers to strengthen them; if such a fort were set on fire, either accidentally or by enemy attack, and if conditions were right, the burning timbers caused the stonework to melt and fuse together and the wall to become distorted (these are known as vitrified forts).

Earthwork defences could be as impressive as stone walls, particularly if the height of the rampart were increased by a timber stockade along its crest and if several lines of rampart and ditch were built.

Hilltops are not the most convenient places to live, and the skyhigh location of a fort such as Eildon Hill North must imply that defence and prestige were the major factors in choosing where to build. Eildon was almost certainly a stronghold of the Votadini, one of the major Celtic tribes of southern Scotland, and therefore a place of great status and the ultimate refuge for lowland members of the tribe, whereas minor chieftains could afford to live closer to the farming land on which their lives depended. Amongst the proud warrior aristocracy of Celtic society, prestige is likely to have ranked almost as high as defence in the design of a fortified farm such as **Rispain Camp** in Wigtown or a small fortified village such as **The Chesters** in East Lothian. It happens that most of the forts in state care are in relatively low-lying situations, simply because their need for protection against modern changes in land-use is greater than that of hilltop forts, but there is, nevertheless, a comprehensive range to be visited.

The **Caterthuns** in Angus represent the classic hilltop location as well as a variety of building methods. Well-named, the **White Caterthun** is crowned by a mass of pale stone, while the **Brown Caterthun** lies beneath a dark mantle of heather. The two forts are only 2.6 km apart, but they are very different and both were in use over very long periods of time. They are amongst the best-preserved forts in Scotland. The basic elements of each are stone-built main ramparts with outer earthworks, but the scale and treatment vary. The **White Caterthun** has a massive spread of stones tumbled from two concentric walls, which in their heyday must have presented a stunning sight—the inner wall alone was some 12 m thick and several metres high. A great hollow in the interior marks the location of a large rock-cut cistern that held the fort's water-supply. Two major outer lines of earthwork defences are still visible. The stone-walled fort on the **Brown Caterthun** is larger in area although not as impressive in scale as the White fort, but it has three outer lines of earthworks with which it

The **White Caterthun** hillfort.

shares an odd feature: causeways apparently marking no fewer than nine entrances. If they were original, it may be that this was no ordinary fort. It is not unknown, however, for an iron age fort to become the traditional location for medieval and later fairs, and some comparable explanation could account for extra breaks in the ramparts.

The fort at **Castlelaw** near Edinburgh is overlooked by higher ground but is nevertheless an impressive defensive work, and excavation has revealed a long history of fortification that is typical of the later 1st millennium BC in south-east Scotland. Originally, in the middle centuries of the 1st millennium, there was a farming community whose houses were enclosed within a

Castlelaw, Midlothian
This low foothill of the Pentlands is mantled by the concentric rings of rampart and ditch of a prestigious iron age fort. The most conspicuous rampart is the middle one of three, and an earth-house was built in its lee, snugly fitted into the innermost ditch.

Castlelaw, Midlothian
This artist's impression of the gateway into the fort, seen from the inside, is based upon the pattern of post-holes found during excavation. The upper part of the wooden tower would have provided an essential look-out post as well as extra protection for the weakest point in the defences, and there are guard-chambers on either side of the gate. Wooden ladders allow access to the top of the rampart and the tower.

stout timber stockade. This was later replaced by an earthen rampart and ditch, with a strong timber gateway controlling access into the fort. Later still, two extra ramparts and ditches were added.

The clearest example of a fort designed for prestige rather than strictly for defence is **The Chesters** in East Lothian. The fort is oval, enclosing a low rise within two ramparts and ditches; access to the entrances at either end is through an impressive set of additional defences, three banks and ditches at one end and five at the other, a formidable entry to negotiate even before the main gate was reached. Yet the whole complex lies at the foot of a higher ridge and the houses inside the fort would have been easy targets for arrows and slingstones launched from above. No excavation has taken place, but the uneven ground inside the fort hints at the remains of houses beneath the turf, and the modern farm nestling close to the ramparts underlines the basic farming economy that links

The Chesters fort seen from the air.

Opposite
Rispain Camp, Wigtown
The major element that survives today is the defences: a deep ditch with the remains of ramparts on either side, forming a rectangular enclosure. It lies on the sloping end of the ridge, and it may be that the V-shaped ditch had as vital a function for drainage as it did for defence.

the two. At several forts there is evidence of occupation continuing, or perhaps beginning again, after the defences had ceased to be regarded as important. This sequence can be seen even without excavation at **The Chesters** and at **Edin's Hall** near Duns in Berwickshire, where surface traces of stone-built houses clearly overlie the earlier ramparts. At **Castlelaw**, Midlothian, someone of economical mind devised a labour-saving way of building an earth-house in the ditch between two ramparts (see page 20).

At the other end of the scale from the defended village community is the small structure that can have protected just one or two families: into this category come the many duns and crannogs of western and central Scotland. The classic dun is the stone-built structure clinging to a rocky knoll, but on Arran there is a beautiful grass-grown dun, for all the world like a medieval motte, at **Torr a' Chaisteal**. Set back from the shore, an isolated knoll was fortified with a thick stone wall and a substantial earthwork across the easiest access-route: only two courses of the dun wall are now visible, but it must have been a most impressive structure, built of large boulders and more than 3 m thick. The interior of the dun, some 8 m in diameter, may have been occupied by a single house, the stronghold perhaps of a chieftain sometime during the last few centuries BC and the first few centuries AD.

A comparable fort is the D-shaped earthwork on **Barsalloch Point** near Monreith in Wigtown, the chord of the D being the steep cliff edge of the promontory, and the whole enclosing only enough land for a small fortified farmstead. The ditch is still impressive, some 10 m wide and 3.5 m deep, and there are eroded ramparts on either side.

Rispain Camp, near Whithorn in Wigtown, is a spectacular example of a fortified iron age farm. Its defences are so well preserved that archaeologists have been misled into believing it to be either a Roman fort or a medieval moated homestead, but excavations have left no doubt that it was built and inhabited between about 100 BC and AD 200 by local Celtic farmers. The name Rispain is thought perhaps to derive from a local equivalent of the Old Welsh word *rhwospen*, meaning 'the chief of the cultivated country', which would certainly be appropriate to this prestigious iron age farm.

Rispain Camp, Wigtown
The entrance is on the downslope side, where there is a broad causeway across the defences; excavation revealed the traces of a timber gateway, which would probably have been connected to a timber stockade running along the top of the inner rampart. There was also evidence of large timber roundhouses inside the enclosure, and this drawing gives an impression of the original appearance of this busy and prosperous farm. Cattle, sheep and pigs were kept, and hunting in the surrounding woodland provided venison; barley and wheat may have been used not just as foods but also, in the case of barley, for brewing alcoholic drink.

Aerial view of the **Ness of Burgi,** Shetland. The turf-covered remains of the blockhouse stand proud, and the roofless cells show up as dark holes. The rectangular cairn (bottom left) is modern and consists of stones cleared from the fort during excavation and consolidation.

Shetland forts

Coastal promontories were popular locations for building forts, taking advantage of natural defences: precipitous cliffs on three sides left only the fourth to be protected by ramparts. A fort that must come close to the ultimate in making use of natural defences is the spectacular **Ness of Burgi** in Shetland: the promontory itself is only barely attached by a narrow rocky neck to the mainland, then there is a rampart enclosing a plateau of good pasture before the fort itself is reached. This lies on a small promontory jutting out from the main promontory and must once have been a daunting sight, its back to the sea and its façade a mass of masonry. A great rampart clad in stone spanned the neck of the promontory, with a ditch on either side and a narrow, forbidding entrance-passage. Beyond it rose a solid, blank-walled building, the only entrance a low, covered passage-way that forced a less than dignified arrival, stooping, into the fort.

Such forts seem to have been a Shetland speciality. The rectangular building inside the rampart has been given the anachronistic name of blockhouse (a term used from the 16th century onwards to describe a fort blocking a strategic point), though it is really a gatehouse, and similar buildings have been found in a promontory situation on Scatness (adjacent to **Ness of Burgi**) and on islands in lochs at **Clickhimin**, near Lerwick, and Huxter on Whalsay. They consist of great blocks of masonry containing corbelled cells on either side of low roofed passages, with a door-check and bar-holes well within the passage. Only at **Clickhimin** did the sequence of fortification continue with the building of a broch, but even there the gatehouse was not dismantled and survives to a height of almost 3 m.

Clickhimin, Shetland

The massive gatehouse presented a blank face to visitors, the only break in the smooth masonry being the entrance. Two oval cells lie within, accessible only from above — were they meant for storage purposes or could they have been pit-prisons?

Brochs

Twice in its history Scotland's response to troubled times has been to build strongly fortified residences for chiefs and wealthy landowners. The medieval response gave us towerhouses; the iron age response gave us brochs. Some 500 brochs have survived, mostly in the north and west, and they are a uniquely Scottish phenomenon; many are now little more than mounds of tumbled stone, but some are still awesome memorials to the determination of their builders.

As an architectural fashion, they were relatively short-lived. They seem to have developed by about 100 BC out of combined traditions of thick-

Mousa, Shetland

Confident in its island fastness, the broch of **Mousa** has survived virtually intact, partly because of its remote location and partly because it was probably one of the tallest brochs built. Its outer defence was a thick stone wall, enclosing the promontory on which it stands, but that has vanished all but for its very foundations.

Right
Mousa
Within the thickness of the wall, the stairway winds up to the top of the broch.

Far Right
Glenelg

walled roundhouses and small stone-built forts, and the need for them seems to have passed by about AD 100, although of course many continued in use for a century or more thereafter. Essentially the broch (from Old Norse *borg*, fort) is a massively built roundhouse grown tall. Not all were as tall as the most famous of brochs on the Shetland island of **Mousa** (still 13 m high and originally at least 15 m), but they were all circular towers, with no windows and normally a single entrance, built with walls exceeding thick at the base and tapering as they rose. In the far north the wall-base is commonly solid stonework, but elsewhere it contains cells and galleries. Common to all brochs is the characteristic hollow-wall construction of the upper part of the tower, for this reduced the weight of the drystone masonry and thus allowed greater height to be achieved safely. Horizontal slabs across the hollow wall-core bonded the inner and outer faces together and allowed a stairway to be created within the wall, leading up to a look-out gallery at the top of the broch.

Right
Dun Telve, Glenelg
Like its neighbour, **Dun Troddan**, part of the broch wall is remarkably well-preserved and stands 10 m high, giving a fine impression of its original forbidding profile.

Far Right
A guard-cell, now open to the sky, leads off from the right-hand side of the entrance passage.

Far Left
Dun Telve
The upper scarcement is visible towards the top of the wall: this probably supported the roof of the timber gallery within the broch.

Left
Dun Troddan
The broch stands in part to a height of 7.6 m, and the well-built inner face shows a distinct scarcement at a low level.

The cells and galleries were probably used for storage, apart from the guard cells sometimes opening off the entrance passage, behind the door. The ground floor of the broch acted as living-room, furnished with slab-built hearth and storage tanks, water-cistern or well, and sleeping accommodation was on a timber gallery lining the upper part of the broch. These have long since rotted away, but excavation has revealed post-holes in the floors of several brochs (the best example is **Dun Troddan**, in Glenelg, where a complete ring of post-holes was found), and there is often a narrow ledge, or scarcement, running round the inner face of the broch wall at a height (between 1.5 m and 3.3 m) that suggests that it supported the horizontal beams of the gallery. The two tallest surviving brochs, **Mousa** and **Dun Telve**, the latter also in Glenelg, close by **Dun Troddan**, have a second ledge higher up which probably supported the roof of the gallery. The broch itself is unlikely to have been roofed, so as to allow light into the interior.

Dun Beag, Skye
Much of the wall of this broch lies downslope as rubble, but what survives shows a high standard of building. There must have been wide views from the original wall-head.

Of the three doorways on the left, the first leads into a round cell, the second is the entrance passage, and the third leads both to a small cell and to a neatly built flight of stairs. The base of the broch is galleried. As at **Dun Carloway** on Lewis, the inhabitants appear to have endured an inconveniently uneven floor.

Dun Dornaigil, Sutherland
Also known as Dun Dornadilla, this broch is one of several that boast an impressive triangular lintel over the entrance.

Like their medieval counterparts, most brochs survive today as gaunt and isolated shells, but, also like towerhouses, most had an outer enclosure, or barmkin, within which lesser domestic buildings might huddle – compare the broch at **Jarlshof** in Shetland with its high-walled courtyard with the towerhouse at **Smailholm** in the Borders with its barmkin. Many of the broch-sites in the far north developed into fortified villages, each dominated by its tower, and the village sometimes outlived the broch.

Vast quantities of artefacts and animal bones have been recovered from excavations of brochs and their associated buildings, although unfortunately it is often now impossible to know exactly where they were found on the site, because so many brochs were cleared out in the 19th century. The situation is rather better with the collections from **Gurness** and **Midhowe** in Orkney, which were excavated in the mid 20th century, and modern excavations at **Howe** in Orkney and **Old Scatness** in Shetland have improved our

Midhowe, Rousay, Orkney
This was a tightly-knit defensive unit with very little space between the broch and its enclosing rampart and ditches. Later houses were built across the inner ditch, and other domestic buildings to the north and west of the broch have been eroded by the sea (the site is now protected by a sea-wall). The rocky shore provided endless building stone.

understanding even more. **Gurness** alone yielded more than 850 artefacts and a vast quantity of broken pottery. Overall the impression is given of an economy based on mixed farming and fishing, local production of pottery, tools and clothing and a taste for exotic imports from the south of Scotland (acquired presumably by honest barter, as loot from raids or as gifts). The latter include items of Roman origin such as the red Samian pottery and bronze ladle from **Midhowe** and the fragment of a glass bowl found at **Clickhimin** which is thought to have been made in Alexandria in Egypt around AD 100.

Discoveries of clay crucibles and moulds, as well as slag, are evidence of the activities of bronzesmiths and blacksmiths, manufacturing bronze jewellery and fittings for weapons (such as knobs for the base of spear-shafts, a mould for which came from **Gurness**) and iron tools. Notable among a wide variety of bone and stone tools are spinning and weaving equipment, querns and grinders for processing grain, stone lamps and, in a lighter vein, bone gaming dice.

Left
The entrance is unusually spacious: with a height of almost 2 m, most people could enter without stooping.

Far Left
Clickhimin, Shetland
Originally on a small rocky island in the loch, **Clickhimin** developed from a farmstead of about 700 BC into a fort, with a massive free-standing gatehouse, towards the end of the millennium. To the fort was then added a broch with a solid wall-base and the unusual feature of two additional entrances. The island was inhabited at least until the mid 1st millennium AD, long after the broch itself had been converted to a domestic roundhouse.

GURNESS

Until 1930, the broch of **Gurness** was hidden beneath a vast grassy mound, but a decade of excavation and consolidation revealed not only a broch and its encircling defences but also a unique complex of domestic buildings dating from broch times and on into the historical Pictish era.

The northern part of the site has suffered from coastal erosion, but it seems likely that originally the outer defences encircled the broch entirely. The main element is a rock-cut ditch, about 4 m wide and up to 2 m deep, its sides faced with drystone walling, and it is accompanied by two outer ramparts. An entrance on the east side lines up with the entrance into the broch, and the pathway between the two was honoured by the buildings that grew up around the broch tower and remains an impressively ordered sight even today.

The broch has survived to a maximum height of only about 3.5 m, owing to stone robbing and collapse, but in a sense its denuded state is a measure of the success of its location, for the site was inhabited on and off for some 900 years, and later builders used the old tower as a convenient quarry. The thick wall-base has a gallery running through it, and the interior of the broch, about 10 m in diameter, is crowded with slab-built cubicles, staircases, hearths and a remarkable well, 4 m deep. Some of these furnishings, including the well, are original and others are later additions.

Aerial view of **Gurness** from the seaward side.

Far Left
The great broch wall has been severely robbed.

Left
Inside the broch.

Far Left and Left
Houses outside the broch.

Gurness is most famous, however, for the village of terraced houses that surrounds the broch. They are somewhat irregular in shape and mostly so large that it is unlikely that they were wholly roofed — better perhaps to think of them as walled yards in which there were smaller roofed buildings and space out-of-doors for working and playing. There are hearths and doorways and slab-lined tanks, and the whole impression is of a busy and flourishing, close-knit community. Here, better than anywhere, it is possible to appreciate the endless variations on what can be achieved with large thin slabs of Orkney flagstones.

A pathway leads to the broch.

The dating evidence available is not very precise but an acceptable sequence seems to be that the broch and its outer defences were built in the 1st century AD, if not earlier, and that the village developed subsequently (the outer walls of the houses encroach upon the great ditch), broch and village together thriving for three or four centuries. There was then a gap of two centuries or so, during which Gurness lay apparently abandoned, the broch and the houses filling with debris, to the extent that the new inhabitants, around AD 600, were able to level the ruins and build their own, quite different, houses on top of the old. All later buildings had to be removed in the course of excavation in order to expose the original village, but one of these Pictish houses has been rebuilt in front of the museum: it consists of a series of small oval rooms built round a central hearth. Part of an oblong house has also been rebuilt; its date is uncertain but it may be a Viking Age longhouse. There was certainly Viking Age activity on the site, because a 9th-century grave and a number of contemporary stray objects have been found.

Gurness is one of eight brochs lining the shores of Eynhallow Sound, four on Mainland and four on Rousay, and the importance of the area seems to have continued into Pictish times, because a marvellous treasure of silver and amber (now, alas, lost) was found buried in the ruins of one of the other brochs.

EDIN'S HALL

Edin's Hall, near Duns in Berwickshire, might be seen as the lowland equivalent of **Gurness**. This is an impressive site about which tantalisingly little is known, apart from the basic sequence of its components: fort, broch and settlement of stone-built houses, all of which can be seen on the ground and, perhaps even more clearly, on the aerial photograph. The broch and some of the houses were dug on several occasions in the 19th century but few finds and little information resulted. Major problems arise from lack of dating evidence. For instance, what was the relationship between the fort and its neighbour on Cockburn Law? A classic hilltop fort caps the Law, high above Edin's Hall lying on its lower slope, and it is difficult to envisage the two as contemporary. If the Edin's Hall fort was built late in the 1st millennium BC, it may not be much older than the broch. The fort was built on the edge of the steep slope that drops away to the Whiteadder Water below, so that one side of the fort at least had some natural defence. Elsewhere there are two ramparts and ditches, with an entrance on the east (confusingly, there are several other breaks across the defences but these are not original). The broch was built in one corner of the fort, and it appears to have its own small walled enclosure round it. This arrangement is reminiscent of forts in southern England where an unusually large house may be set apart within its own enclosure, and where the clear implication is that of special status. It is possible that at Edin's Hall the broch represents the chief's house rebuilt in a new and somewhat alien fashion.

Edin's Hall from the air. The thick-walled broch can be seen to the left, within the oval fort.

Far Left
The remains of the broch.

Left
The broch entrance with its guard cell.

Not surprisingly, the broch is unusual compared with northern examples. With an internal diameter of almost 17 m within a wall 5 to 6 m thick, it is very large for a broch, but it does possess a number of classic broch features including mural cells. In its restored state, the wall is almost 2 m high, and, while it may originally have been twice that height, it seems unlikely that it was ever a tall tower. Nevertheless, it was still sufficiently impressive in late medieval times to have earned the name 'Odin's Hall'.

The entrance passage, almost 5 m long, is checked about halfway along for a door, behind which there is a guard cell on either side. Three larger cells within the wall can be entered from the courtyard, one with a stairway leading upwards.

Apart from the broch, a number of circular buildings and walls fills the rest of the fort interior, some overlying the old defences. A passage-way through these later buildings leads from the fort-entrance towards the gateway into the broch-enclosure, suggesting, as at **Gurness**, that the broch was still in use during the development of this village. Internally, one of the houses is almost as large as the broch itself and twice the size of the rest of the village, again hinting at a special social or functional status.

Below Left
Cells built within the broch wall.

Below
The large house in the foreground may have belonged to a chieftain.

Broch of Mousa, Shetland
Centuries after its original inhabitants had abandoned it, the old broch gave shelter and protection to runaway Norse lovers in AD 1153, withstanding attack by their pursuers.

FROM PREHISTORY INTO HISTORY

THE Roman presence in Scotland had little visible effect upon the homes of the native inhabitants, except perhaps in the negative sense that some may have been forced to leave or may have abandoned their homes as being too close for comfort to the Roman military network. The influence of Roman activities in southern and central Scotland between the late 1st century and the early 3rd century AD was felt more in social and political spheres. Contact with the Romans brought new and exotic items in to powerful native households: fine red tableware known as Samian pottery, glass vessels, Roman coins (perhaps for their curiosity value rather than as currency), bronze jewellery, all diplomatic gifts or bartered in exchange for furs, woollen cloth, provisions, slaves and the famous Caledonian bears. Artefacts of Roman origin have been found in native farms and villages throughout Scotland, even on the western and northern fringes. The discovery of native iron age pottery, a Roman brooch, and sherds of Samian ware on **Edinburgh Castle** rock confirms the presence of the iron age fort that must surely have preceded the medieval castle.

In political terms, the presence of the Roman army was an external threat that transcended local inter-tribal jealousies and brought rival factions together to face the common enemy. This enforced sense of unity could well explain why brochs became defunct architectural dinosaurs during the 2nd and 3rd centuries. Ultimately, tribal unity led to the federation known to the Romans as the Picts, the ferocious 'barbarians' who harassed the garrisons of Hadrian's Wall and even further south during the final years of the Roman occupation of Britain.

Tribal unity remained long after the Romans left Britain. By the 6th century AD, a Pictish kingdom had emerged that embraced the whole of Scotland north of the Forth and Clyde valleys, apart from the area of modern Argyll that had been settled by Scots from Ireland. The remains of Pictish houses have been found overlying several abandoned broch villages in the far north, notably **Gurness** in Orkney, bringing these essentially prehistoric monuments into the realms of history. It is even possible that the great neolithic sanctuaries were still venerated: excavation at the **Stones of Stenness** uncovered a small pit inside the circle that had been dug in the 6th century AD, for what purpose is now obscure, but it contained burnt grain.

Even the Vikings have left their mark on some prehistoric monuments. Certainly two brochs, and probably more, were used as refuges by the Norsemen (**Mousa** in Shetland and **Dun Carloway** in Lewis), and runic inscriptions were carved inside the great neolithic tomb of **Maes Howe** in the 12th century. Bjorn, who carved his name in runes on the **Ring of Brodgar**, was not alone in his awareness of the prehistoric past of his adopted land.

Carn Liath, Sutherland
Perhaps because its location lacks natural defensive qualities, this broch has a particularly thick and solid wall and is surrounded by a stout outer wall. Between the two, houses once crowded together, the earliest contemporary with the broch; later rebuilding continued after the tower had gone out of use.

A stone-lined passage-way leads from the outer wall to the broch entrance, and there are stone checks for a wooden door in the passage as well as in the broch. The passage was originally roofed over, and some of the flat lintel-slabs were still in position in the 19th century when the site was cleared out.

FURTHER READING

Exploring Scotland's Heritage is a series of eight regional guides to monument of all periods, including detailed direction on how to find them, published by The Stationery Office and the Royal Commission on the Ancient and Historical Monuments of Scotland. In addition, many prehistoric monuments have individual guide-books or leaflet published by Historic Scotland.

The following selection of general books will provide useful background reading:

I Armit, *Celtic Scotland*, London 1997.

P J Ashmore, *Neolithic and Bronze Age Scotland*, London 1996.

D V Clarke, T G Cowie and A Foxon, *Symbols of Power at the Time of Stonehenge*, Edinburgh 1985.

K J Edwards and I B M Ralston, *Scotland: environment and archaeology*, Aberdeen 1997.

N Fojut and D Pringle, *The Ancient Monuments of Shetland*, Edinburgh 1993.

N Fojut, D Pringle and B Walker, *The Ancient Monuments of the Western Isles*, Edinburgh 1994.

A and G Ritchie, *Scotland: an Oxford Archaeological Guide*, Oxford 1998.

A Ritchie and G Ritchie, *The Ancient Monuments of Orkney*, Edinburgh 1999.

G Ritchie, *Brochs of Scotland*, Aylesbury 1998.

ACKNOWLEDGEMENTS

We are indebted to the following institutions and individuals for permission to reproduce photographs:

Royal Commission on the Ancient and Historical Monument of Scotland, Crown Copyright (pp 5, 16, 19, 41); Museum of Scotland, courtesy of the Trustees of the National Museums of Scotland (pp 8, 14, 28, 42, 43, back cover); John Hedges (p 27); Ian A G Shepherd (pp 27, 68); Michael Brooks (p 9); Jean Comrie (p 29); Graham Ritchie (pp 6, 55, 71).

Reconstruction drawings were kindly provided by David Pollock (pp 33, 63, 64) and Norman Mowat (Scottish Buildings Study Group) (pp 10, 21).

The Ring of Brodgar, Orkney
'The view of the Circle of Loda at a distance', by John Frederick Millar, 1775, by courtesy of The British Library.

Index of Places Mentioned in the Text

References to pages with illustrations are given in bold

Index to Map

Printed in Scotland by Scotprint, Musselburgh.